HOW CAN I PLAY THE MODERN CHORDS AS DEMANDED IN ORCHESTRATIONS WITH A CLEAR POWERFUL STYLE?

This is the one predominant question in the minds of ambitious Guitarists today.

Having realized the great need for a system which would produce maximum power with minimum effort, I searched for the most powerful chord that had no repeated voicing and I proceeded to alter it.

The amazing results prompted further research, and gradually brought about the completion of this system which has been adopted by many top flight Guitarists.

Rapid chord progressions can be played with a minimum of movement, thus eliminating the need of continually glancing back and forth, from the printed page to the fingerboard.

The system has been carefully graded, and it is essential to thoroughly master each successive chapter.

A few ultra modern chords not shown in the regular forms throughout the book may be found by consulting the "Summary For Reference", beginning on page 44.

All chords as used in this system are full bodied, powerful in tone and evenly balanced throughout.

Good Luck and Musical Success

To Access the Onine Video Go To:
www.melbay.com/93214V or
dv.melbay.com/93214 - Video Download

3 4 5 6 7 8 9 0

© 1973, 2003 BY MEL BAY PUBLICATIONS, INC., PACIFIC, MO 63069.
ALL RIGHTS RESERVED. INTERNATIONAL COPYRIGHT SECURED. B.M.I. MADE AND PRINTED IN U.S.A.
No part of this publication may be reproduced in whole or in part, or stored in a retrieval system, or transmitted in any form or by any means, electronic, mechanical, photocopy, recording, or otherwise, without written permission of the publisher.

Visit us on the Web at www.melbay.com — E-mail us at email@melbay.com

Contents

The Major Chords	3
Inversions — Majorette	4
Minor Chords — Inversions	5
Minorology — Major to Relative Minor	6
The Dominant Seventh Chord	7
Inversions — Exercises	8
Etudes One, Two and Three	9
Etude Four	10
Etude Five	11
Modulation	12
The Minor Seventh Chord	13
Exercises	14
The 7♭5 Chord	15
Exercises and Etude	16
The 7♯5 Chord	17
Exercises and Etude	18
The Major Seventh Chord	19
The Major Sixth Chord	21
Exercise Etude & Another Major Sixth (exercises)	22
The Minor Sixth Chord — Exercises	23
Exercises and Etude	24
The Diminished Chord	25
Etudes	26
The Ninth Chord	28
The Augmented Chord	27
Exercises, Seventh to Ninth	29
The Minor Ninth Chord	30
The 9♯5 Chord	31
Exercises	32
the 9♭5 Chord	33
Exercises	34
The Major Ninth Chord	35
Exercises	36
The 7♭9 Chord	37
Exercises	38
The Augmented Ninth Chord	39
The Eleventh Chord	40
Exercises	41
The Thirteenth Chord	42
The 13♭9 Chord	43
The 6/9 Chord	44
Summary of Reference	45

The Major Chords

The following major forms have been selected for obtaining the best power and rhythm in modern orchestral playing. The forms are movable and should be practiced from the first to the tenth fret.

The fret location is determined by the first finger. In form [1] the first finger must barre all six strings.

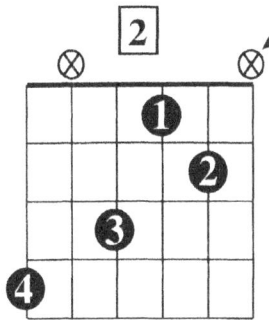

Frets	1	2	3	4	5	6	7	8	9	10
Chords	F	F♯ or G♭	G	A♭	A	B♭	B	C	C♯ or D♭	D

Note: Each Form must be thoroughly mastered before proceeding to the next.

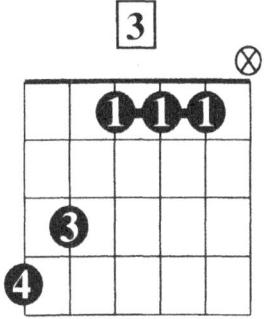

Deaden

Frets	1	2	3	4	5	6	7	8	9	10
Chords	C♯ or D♭	D	E♭	E	F	F♯ or G♭	G	A♭	A	B♭

The Sign ⊗ means **Deadened String**. This is done by allowing the unused part of the left hand to touch the strings just enough to kill the sound.
All Six Strings Will Be Strummed.

Frets	1	2	3	4	5	6	7	8	9	10
Chords	A♭	A	B♭	B	C	D♭ or C♯	D	E♭	E	F

The first string is deadened.
Note that the 2nd finger is not used.

Questions	Answers
What form do we use to play the following chords?	
B♭ on the 6th fret?	Form [1]
E♭ on the 3rd fret?	Form [2]
C on the 5th fret?	Form [3]
D♭ on the 1st fret?	Form [2]
A♭ on the 4th fret?	Form [1]
B on the 4th fret?	Form [3]

After you have memorized the above **Three Major Forms** you are ready to memorize the **Inversions**, as shown on the next page.

Inversions

C Chord* (*This Form is not movable, it is used only at the first fret)

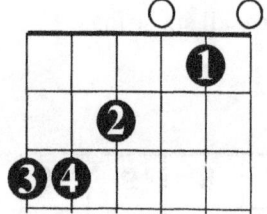

Chords	C			F	
Forms	C*	3	1	1	2
Frets	1	5	8	1	5

Chords	B♭			E♭			A♭			D♭			G♭ or F#	
Forms	3	1	2	2	3	1	3	1	2	2	3	1	1	2
Frets	3	6	10	3	8	11	1	4	8	1	6	9	2	6

Chords	B			E		A			D			G	
Forms	3	1	2	3		3	1	2	2	3	1	1	2
Frets	4	7		4	9	2	5	9	2	7	10	3	7

Majorette

This Study is in Orchestration Style and must be played in strict rhythm.

Mel Bay

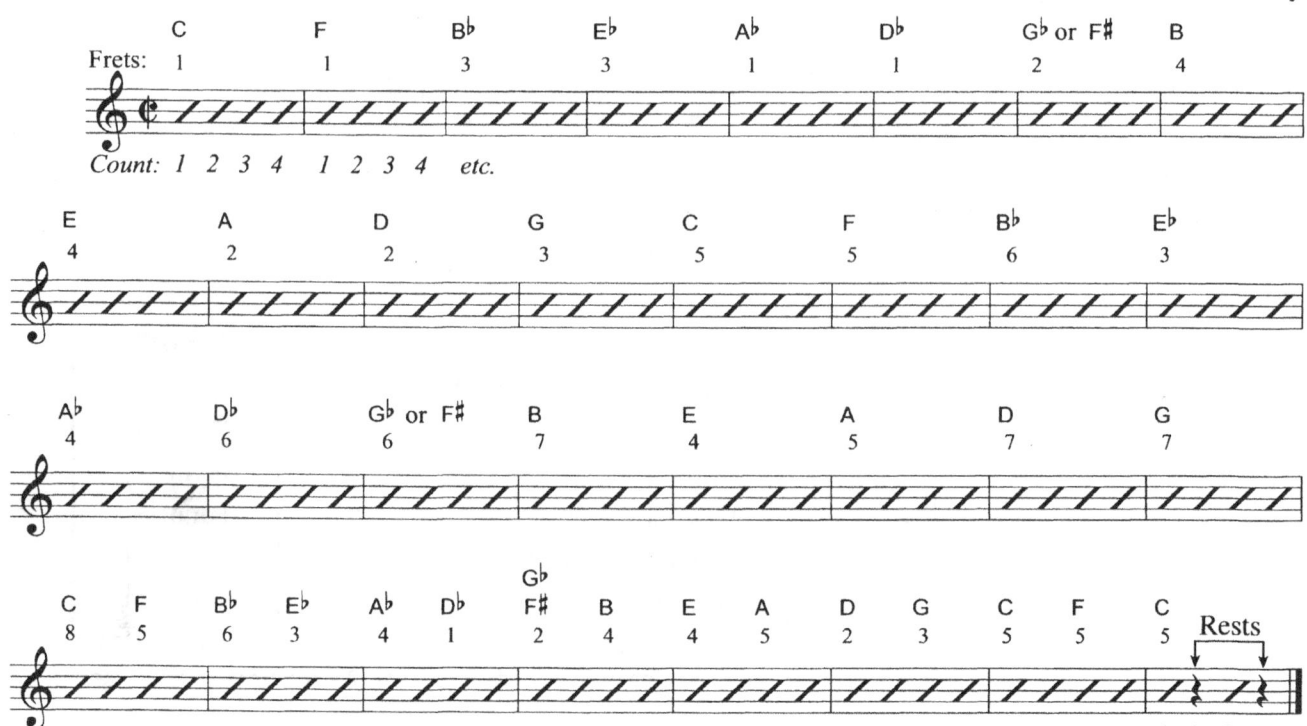

The Minor Chords

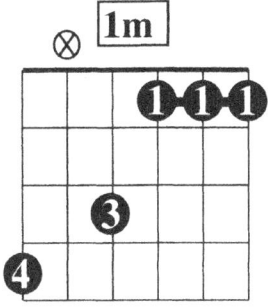

Frets	1	2	3	4	5	6	7	8
Chords	Fm	F#m or G♭m	Gm	A♭m or G#m	Am	B♭m	Bm	Cm

The fifth string is deadened.

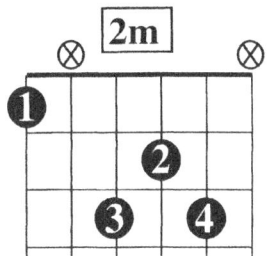

Frets	1	2	3	4	5	6	7	8
Chords	Dm	E♭m or D#m	Em	Fm	G♭m or F#m	Gm	A♭m or G#m	Am

The 1st and 5th strings are deadened.

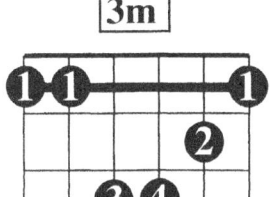

Frets	1	2	3	4	5	6	7	8
Chords	B♭m	Bm	Cm	D♭m or C#m	Dm	E♭m or D#m	Em	Fm

Chords	Cm			Fm			B♭m			E♭m	
Forms	3m	1m	2m	1m	2m	3m	3m	1m	2m	2m	3m
Frets	3	8	11	1	4	8	1	6	9	2	6

Chords	A♭m			D♭m or C#m		G♭m or F#m			Bm	
Forms	1m	2m	3m	3m	1m	1m	2m	3m	3m	1m
Frets	4	7	11	4	9	2	5	9	2	7

Chords	Em		Am		Dm		Gm		
Forms	2m	3m	1m	2m	2m	3m	1m	2m	3m
Frets	3	7	5	8	1	5	3	6	10

Note: For best results in orchestrations, range your chords from 1st to 8th frets.

Minorology

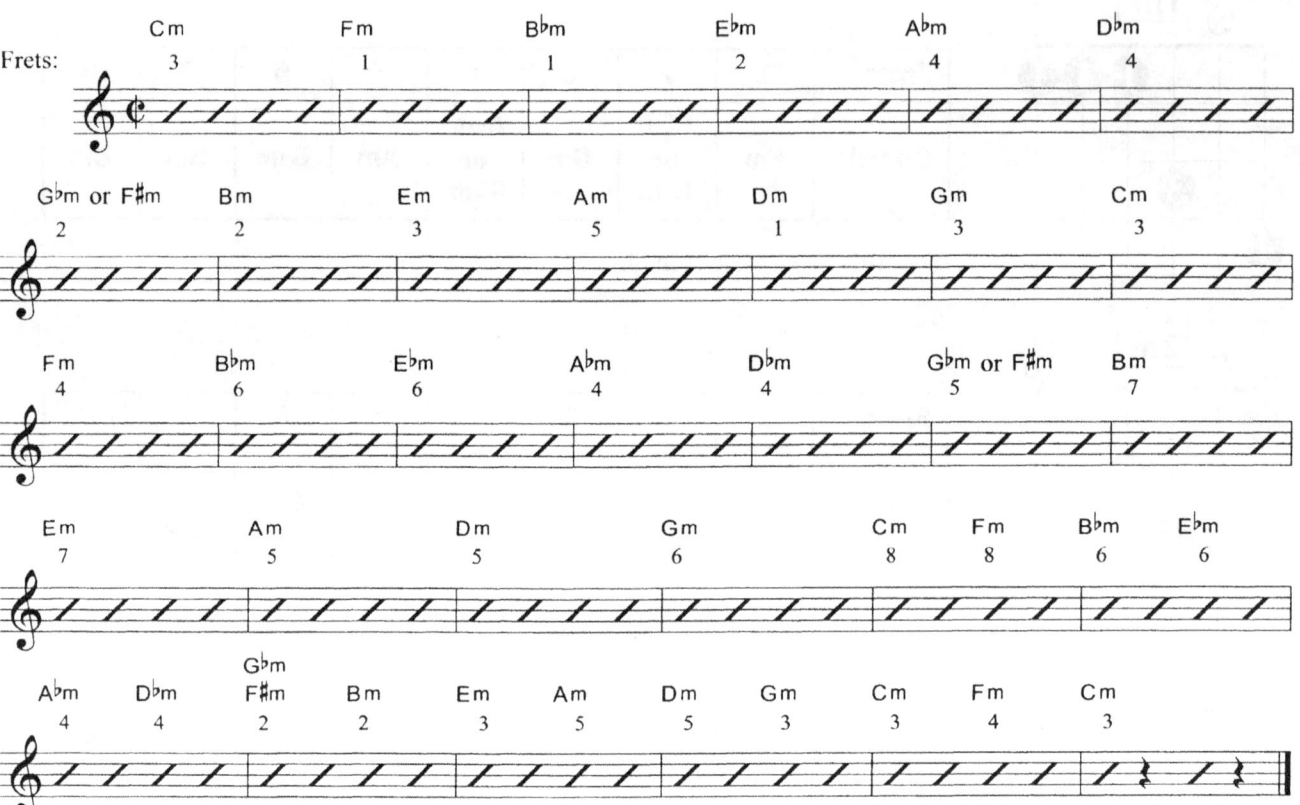

Major to Relative Minor

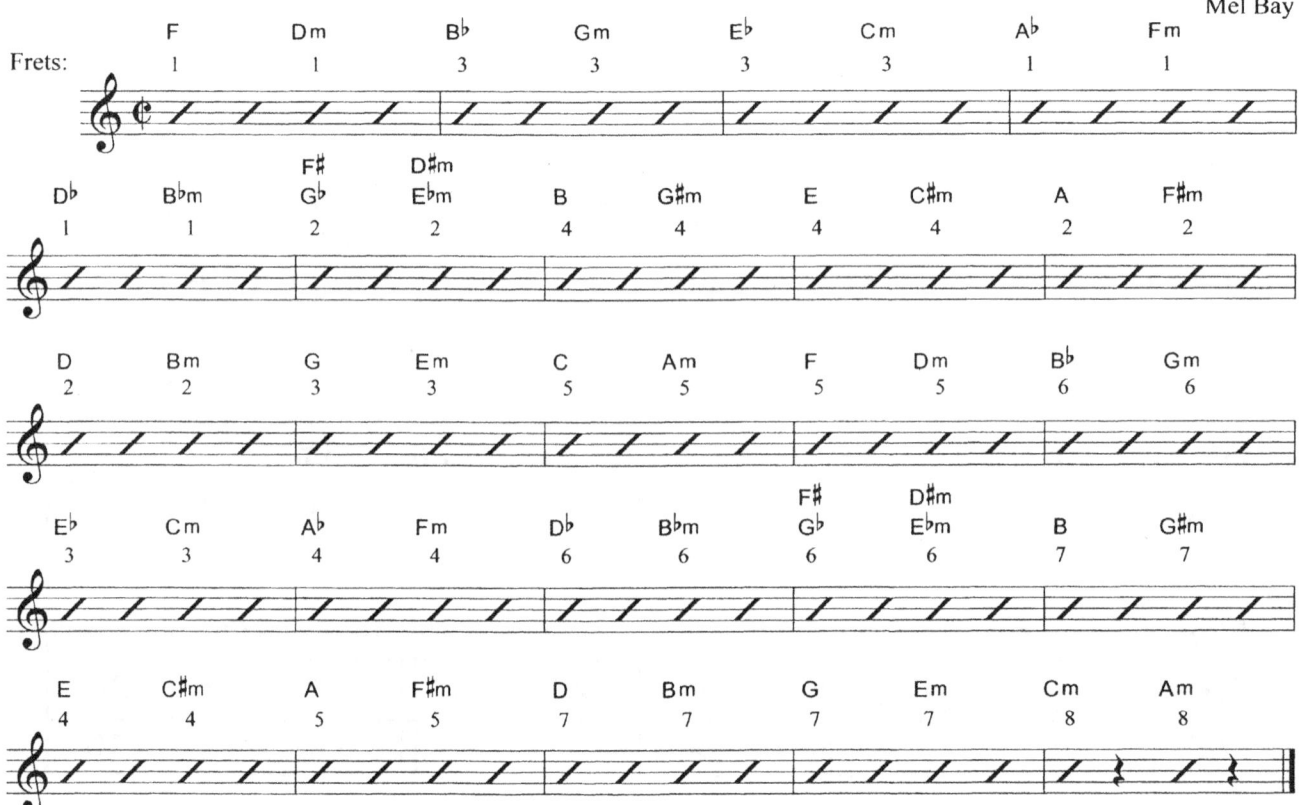

The Dominant Seventh Chord

The 7th chords in this system are played on the ② ③ ④ and ⑥ strings.
The ① and ⑤ strings are deadened, but all six are strummed.
The root of the 7th chord is indicated by the ◆, coincidentally all roots are held with the first finger.
The forms* are numbered I⁷, III⁷, VII⁷.

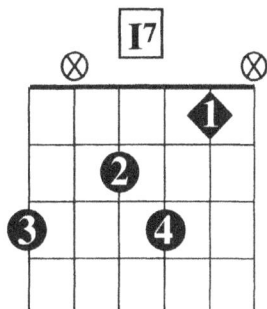

Frets	1	2	3	4	5	6	7	8	9	10
Chords	C7	C#7 or Db7	D7	Eb7 or D#7	E7	F7	F#7 or Gb7	G7	Ab7 or G#7	A7

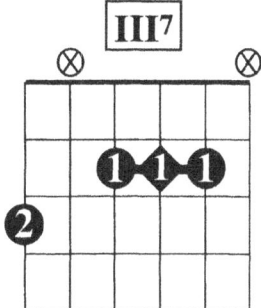

Frets	1	2	3	4	5	6	7	8	9	10
Chords	Ab7	A7	Bb7	B7	C7	Db7 or C#7	D7	Eb7	E7	F7

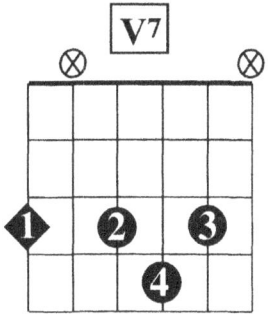

Frets	1	2	3	4	5	6	7	8	9	10
Chords	F7	F#7 or Gb7	G7	Ab7 or G#7	A7	Bb7	B7	C7	Db7 or C#7	D7

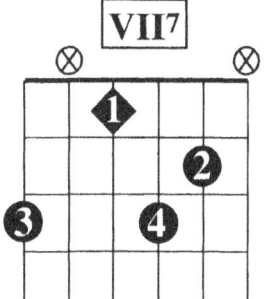

Frets	1	2	3	4	5	6	7	8	9	10
Chords	Eb7	E7	F7	F#7 or Gb7	G7	Ab7 or G#7	A7	Bb7	B7	C7

*The Roman numerals I, III, V, and VII correspond to the chord intervals in the highest voice, namely: root, 3rd, 5th, and 7th. Form I⁷ has the root of the chord on top, form III⁷ 3rd on top, V⁷ 5th on top, and VII⁷ 7th on top.

Inversions

Chords	C7				F7				B♭7			
Forms	I7	III7	V7	VII7	V7	VII7	I7	III7	III7	V7	VII7	I7
Frets	1	5	8	10	1	3	6	10	3	6	8	11

Chords	E♭7 or D♯7				A♭7 or G♯7				D♭7 or C♯7			
Forms	VII7	I7	III7	V7	III7	V7	VII7	I7	I7	III7	V7	VII7
Frets	1	4	8	11	1	4	6	9	2	6	9	11

Chords	G♭7 or F♯7				B7				E7			
Forms	V7	VII7	I7	III7	III7	V7	VII7		VII7	I7	III7	V7
Frets	2	4	7	11	4	7	9		2	5	9	12

Chords	A7				D7				G7			
Forms	III7	V7	VII7	I7	I7	III7	V7		V7	VII7	I7	
Frets	2	5	7	10	3	7	10		3	5	8	

Exercise Using Forms I7 and V7

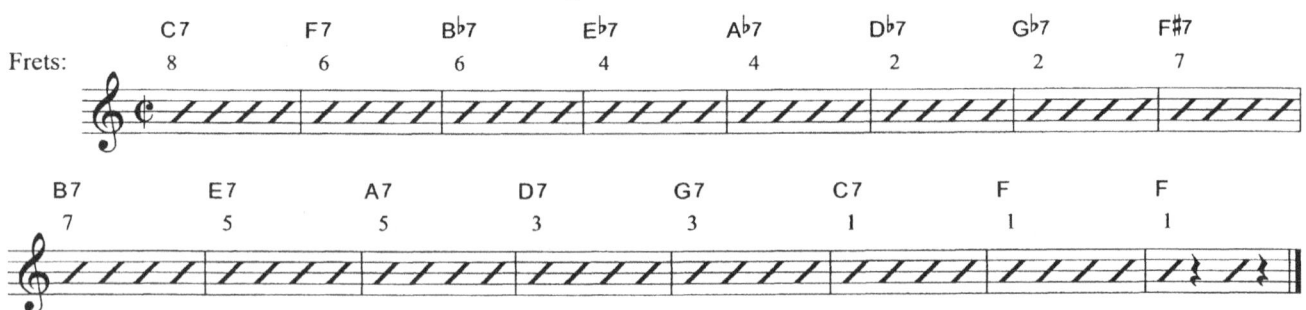

Exercise Using Forms III7 and VII7

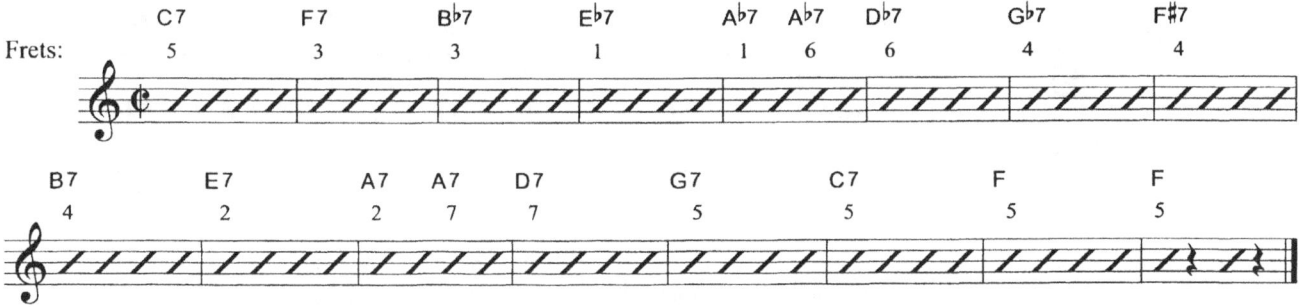

Etude One
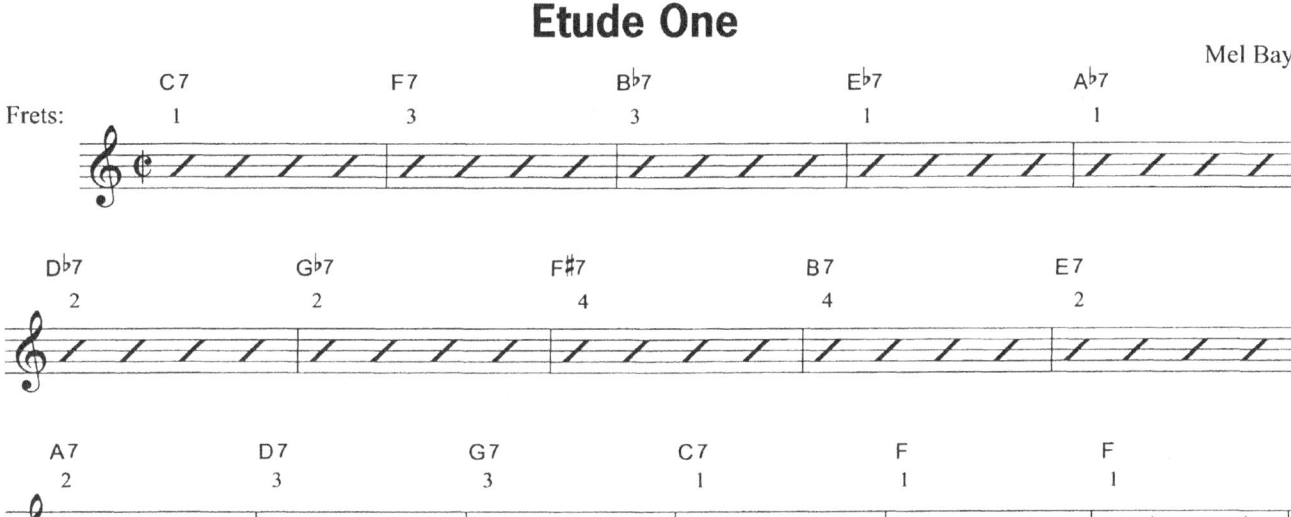

Etude Two
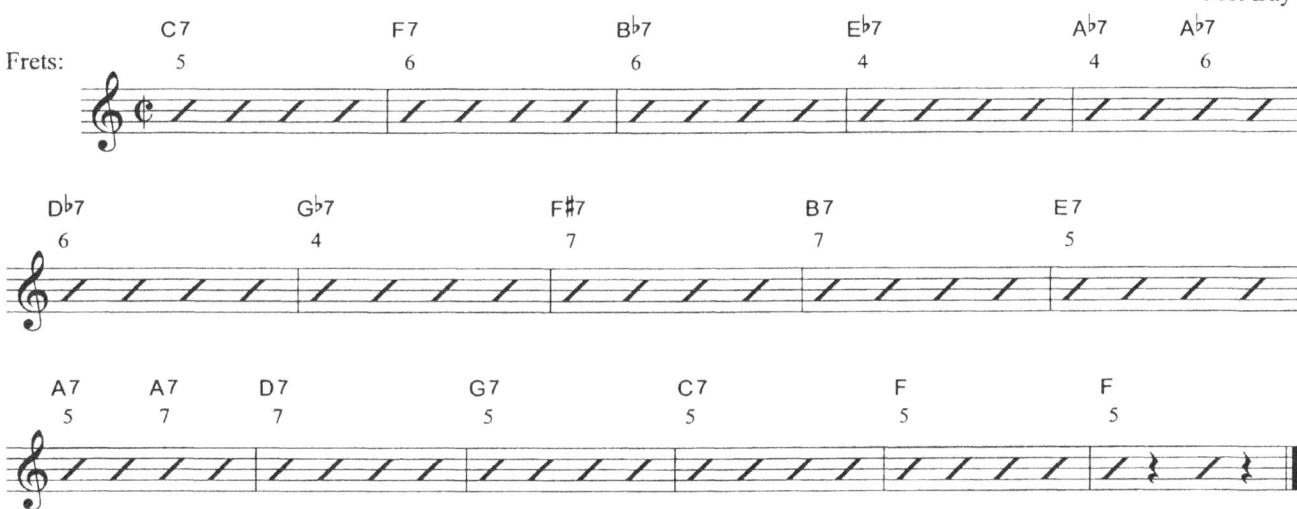

Etude Three
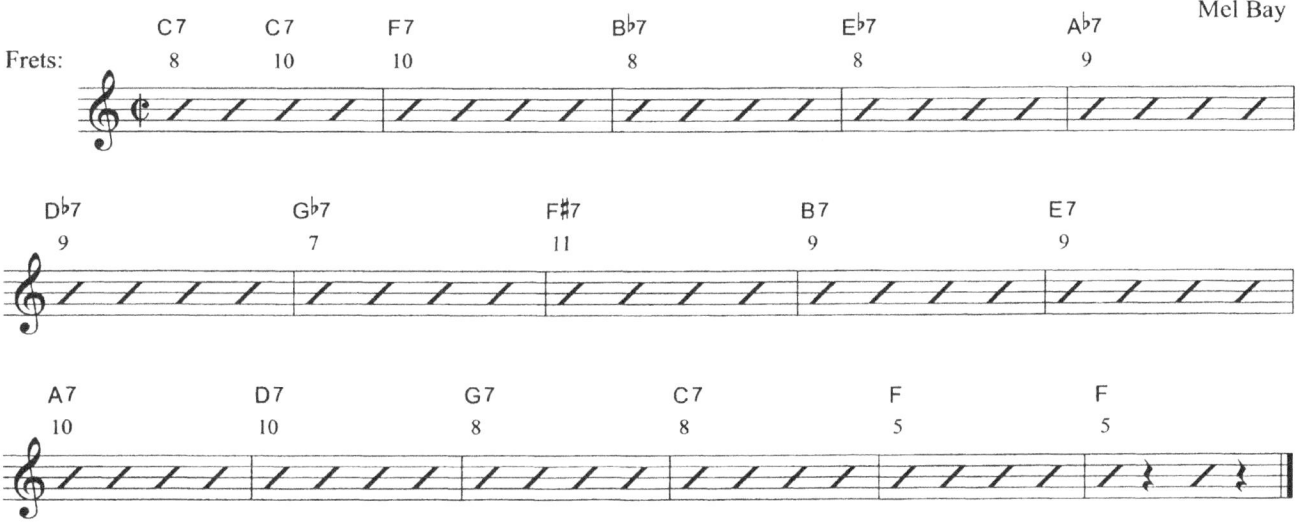

Etude Four

Mel Bay

| Frets: | C 1 | E7 2 | A7 2 | D7 3 | G7 3 | C 1 | C7 1 | F 1 |

| A7 2 | D7 3 | G7 3 | C7 1 | F 1 | F7 3 | B♭ 3 | D7 3 |

| G7 3 | C7 1 | F7 3 | B♭ 3 | B♭7 3 | E♭ 3 | G7 3 | C7 1 |

| F7 3 | B♭7 3 | E♭ 3 | E♭7 1 | A♭ 1 | C7 1 | F7 3 | B♭7 3 |

| E♭7 1 | A♭ 1 | A♭7 1 | D♭ 1 | F7 3 | B♭7 3 | E♭7 1 | A♭7 1 |

| D♭ 1 | D♭7 2 | G♭ 2 | B♭7 3 | E♭7 1 | A♭7 1 | D♭7 2 | G♭ 2 |

| F#7 4 | B 4 | D#7 4 | G#7 4 | C#7 2 | F#7 2 | F#7 4 | B 4 | B7 4 |

| E 4 | G#7 4 | C#7 2 | F#7 2 | F#7 4 | B7 4 | E 4 | E7 2 | A 2 |

| C#7 2 | F#7 2 | F#7 4 | B7 4 | E7 2 | A 2 | A7 2 | D 2 | F#7 4 |

| B7 4 | E7 2 | A7 2 | D 2 | D7 3 | G 3 | B7 4 | E7 2 |

| A7 2 | D7 3 | G 3 | G7 3 | C 1 | E7 2 | A7 2 | D7 3 | G7 3 | C 1 |

Etude Five

Mel Bay

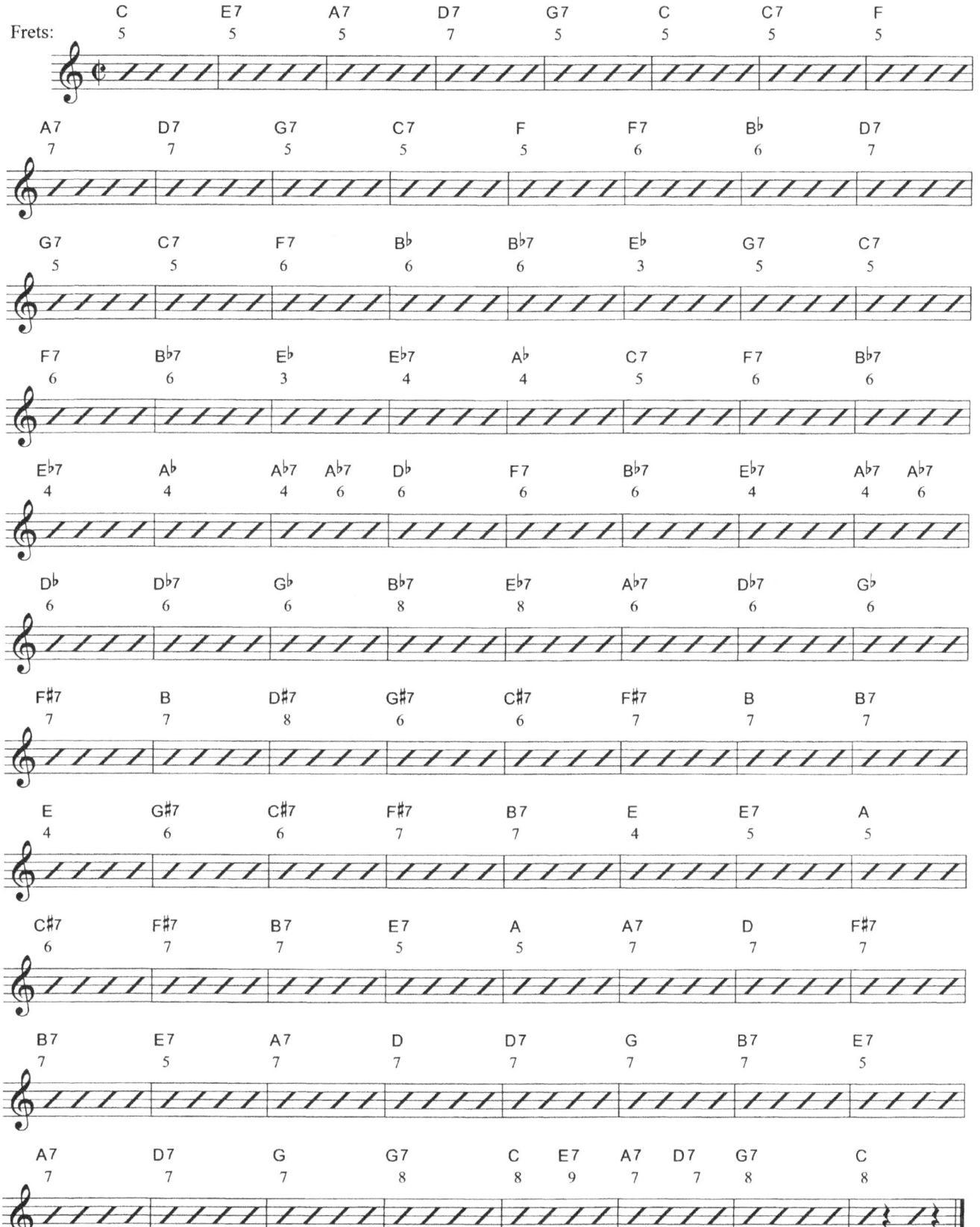

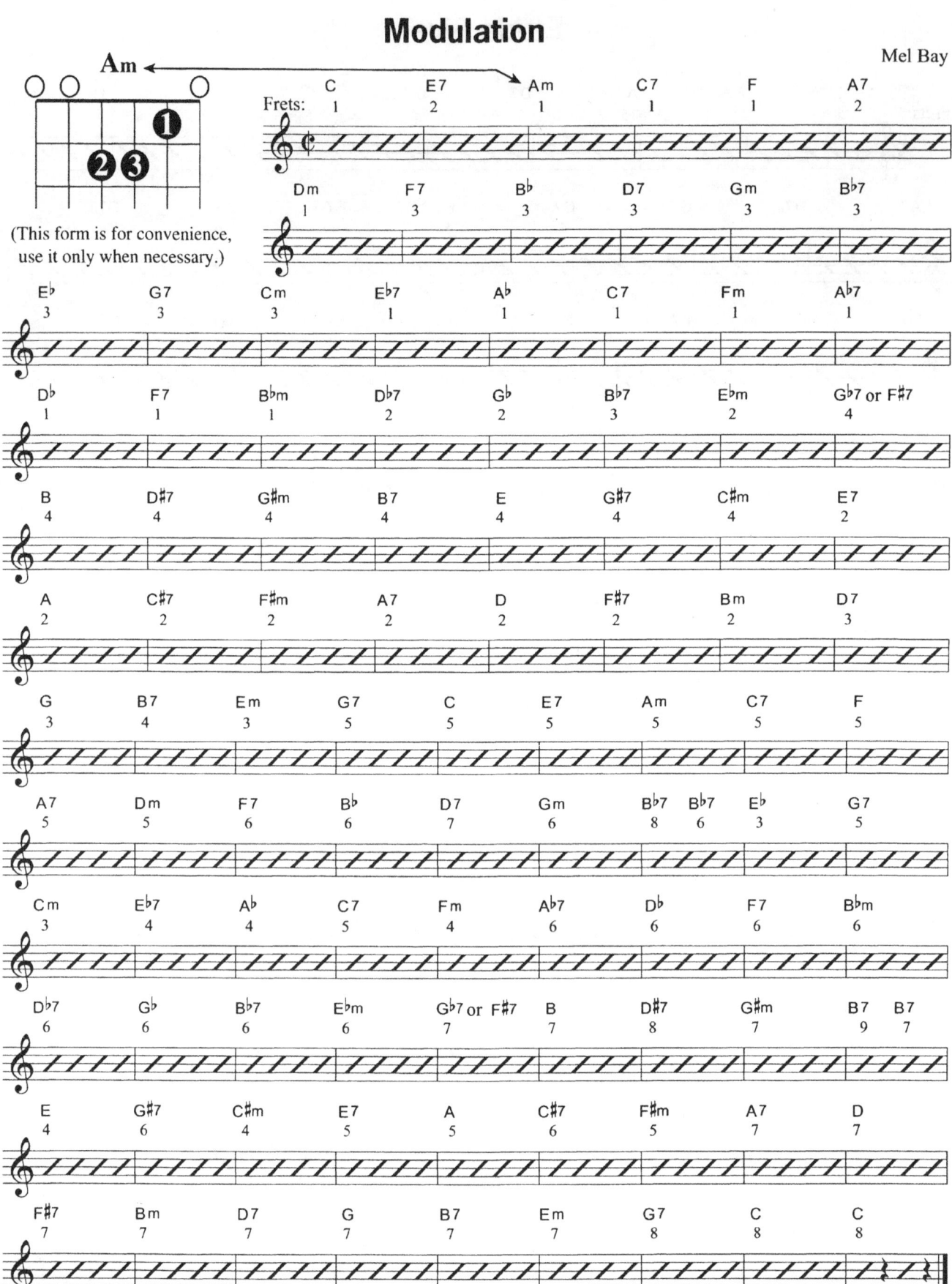

The Minor Seventh Chord

Symbol (m7) = minor 7th

This is one of the most important chords in modern music.

It is made by lowering the 3rd of the dominant seventh chord a half step, or one fret.

The 3rd is indicated by the diamond (◆).

The "X" in the minor seventh forms shows the position of the 3rd before lowering.

Practice these forms until thoroughly mastered

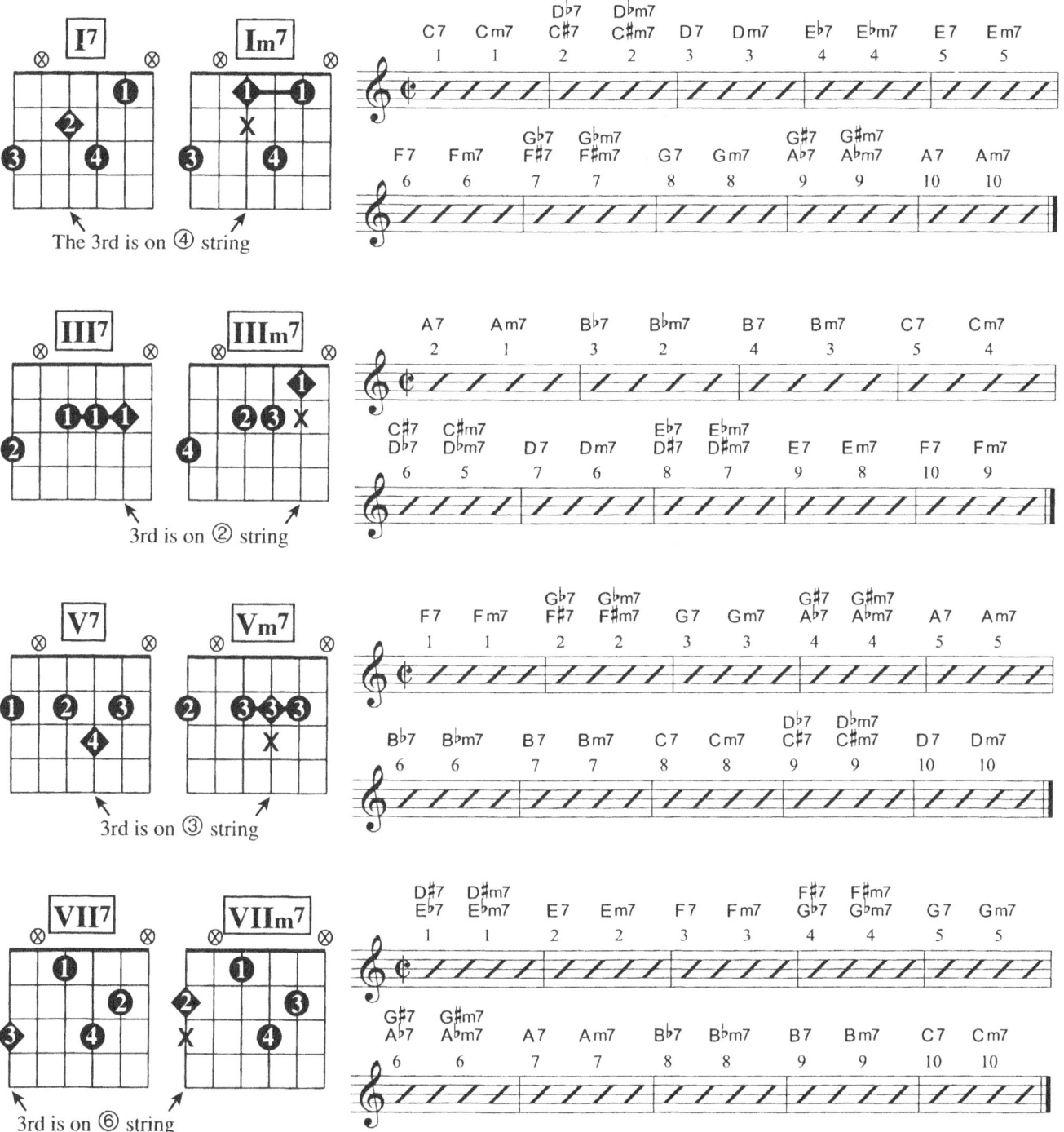

The 7♭5 Chord

This important chord is made by lowering the 5th of the dominant 7th chord one fret. The diamond (♦) indicates the 5th, the "**X**" in the 7♭5 form shows the former position of the 5th.

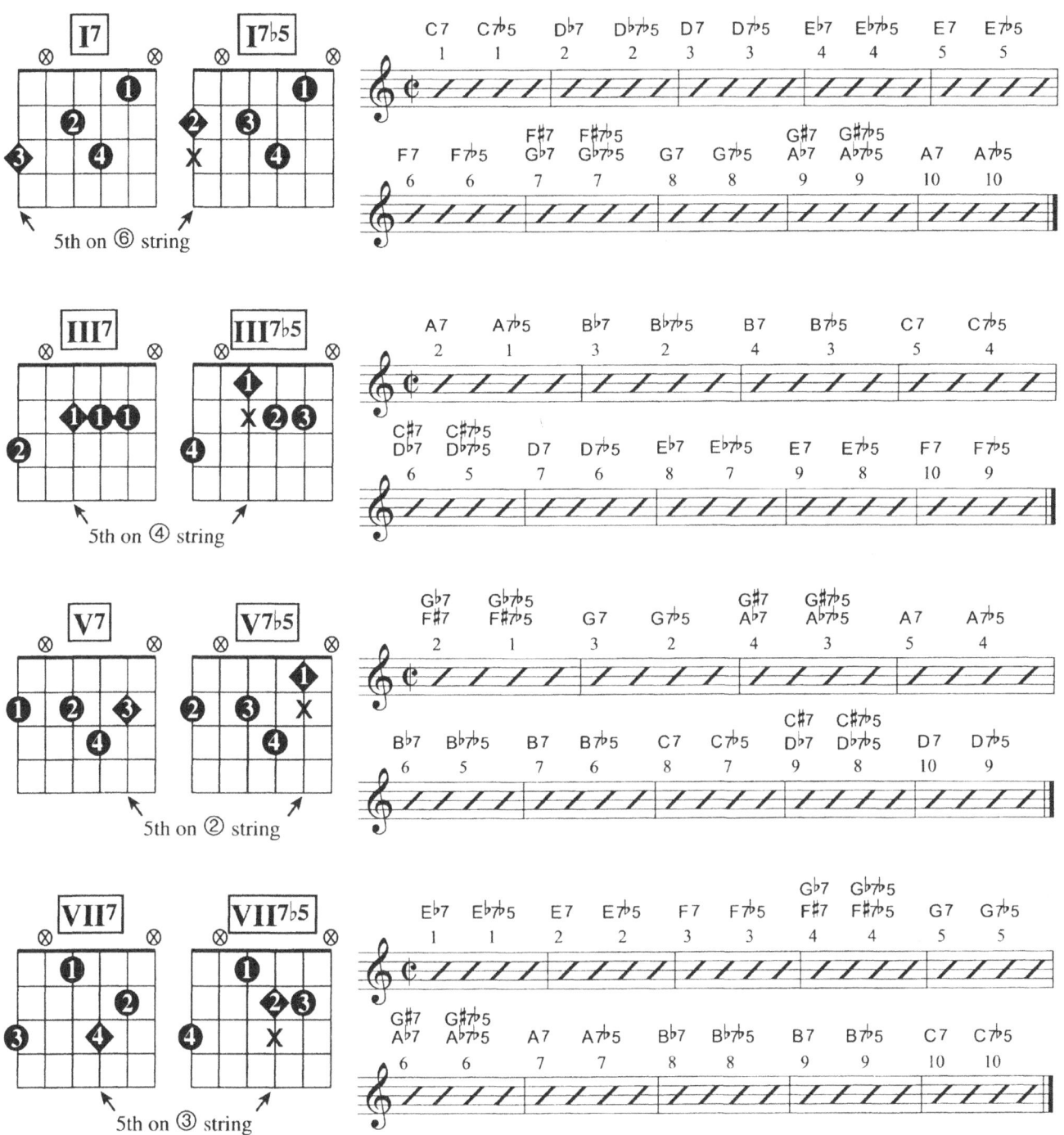

Note that the forms I7♭5 and V7♭5 are identical.
Forms III7♭5 and VII7♭5 are also identical.
To avoid mental confusion always refer to the dominant 7th form from which each 7♭5 form is taken.

Exercise Employing Forms I and V

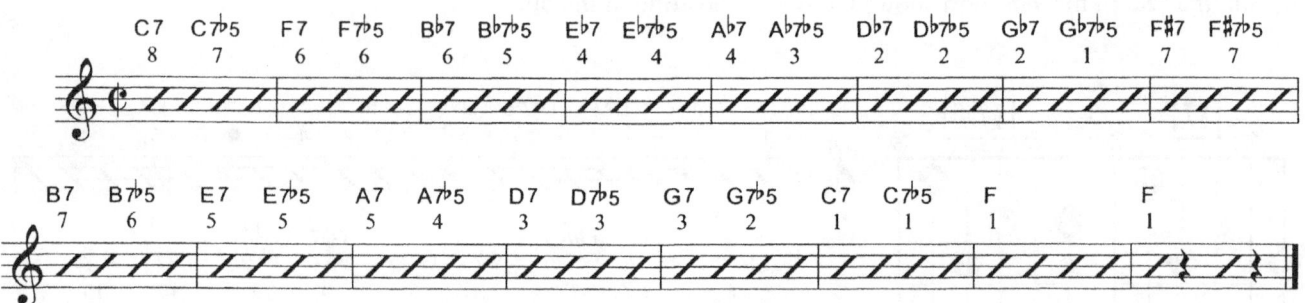

Exercise Employing Forms III and VII

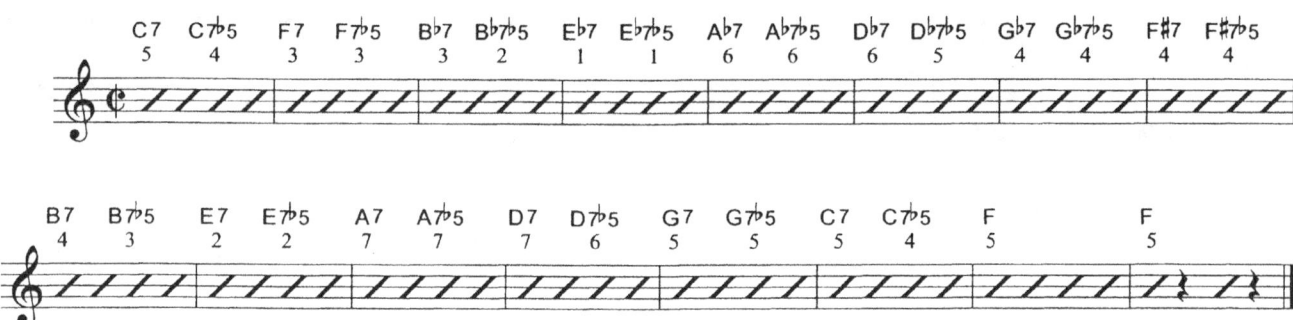

Etude Six

Mel Bay

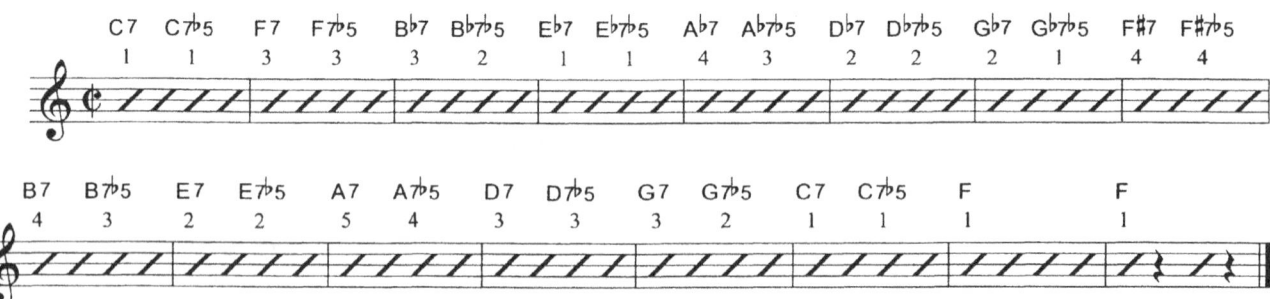

Etude Seven

Mel Bay

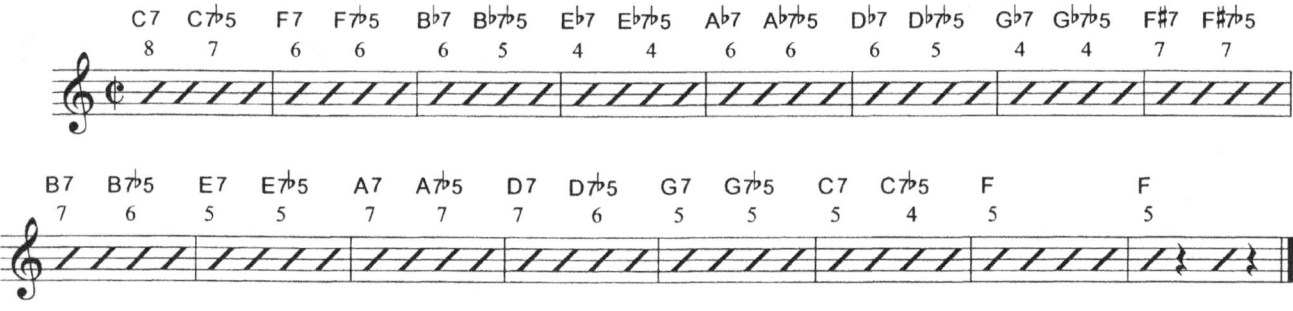

The 7♯5 Chord

This chord is made by raising the 5th of the dominant 7th chord one fret.

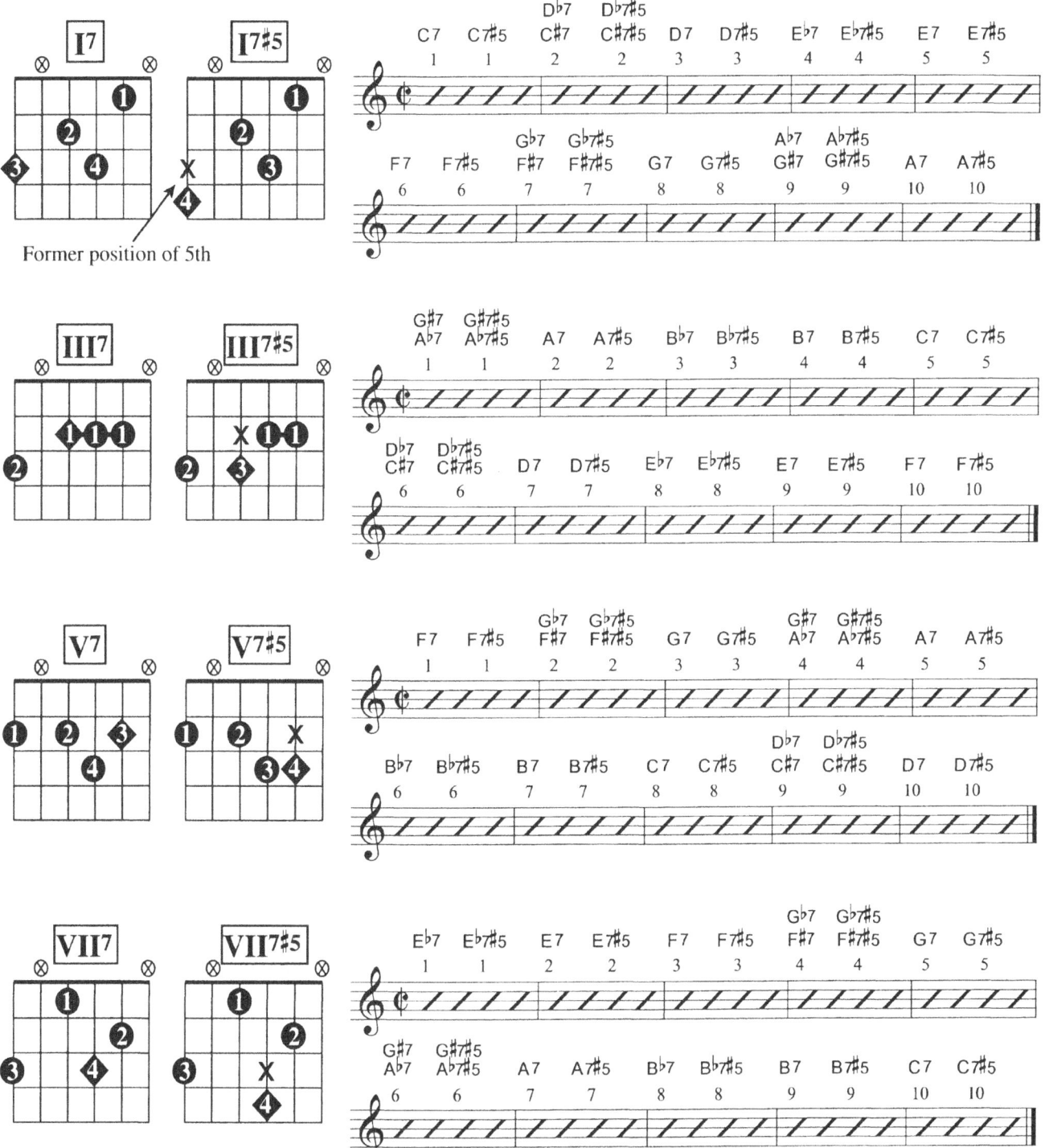

Former position of 5th

Exercise – Forms I and V

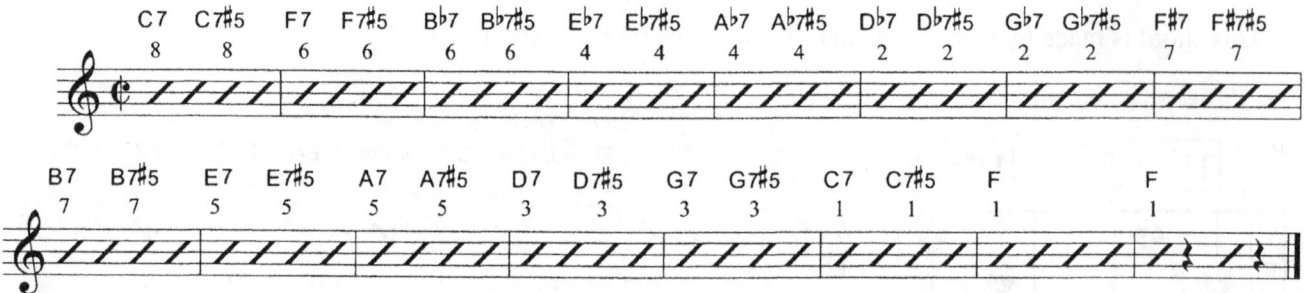

Exercise – Forms III and VII

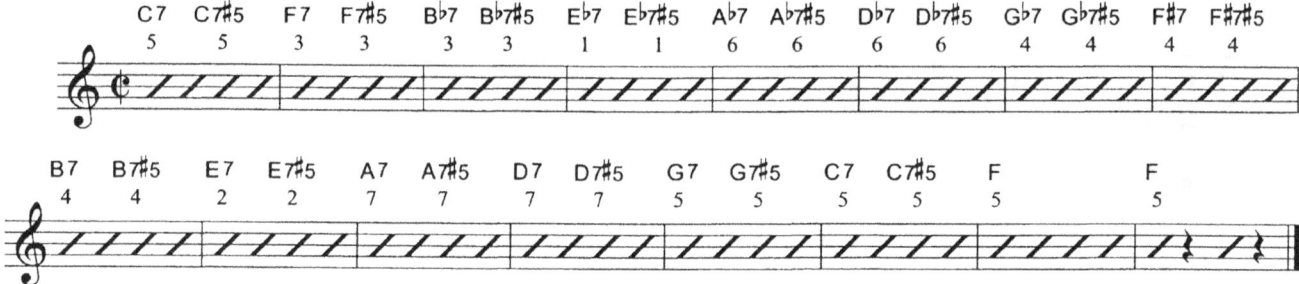

Etude Eight

Mel Bay

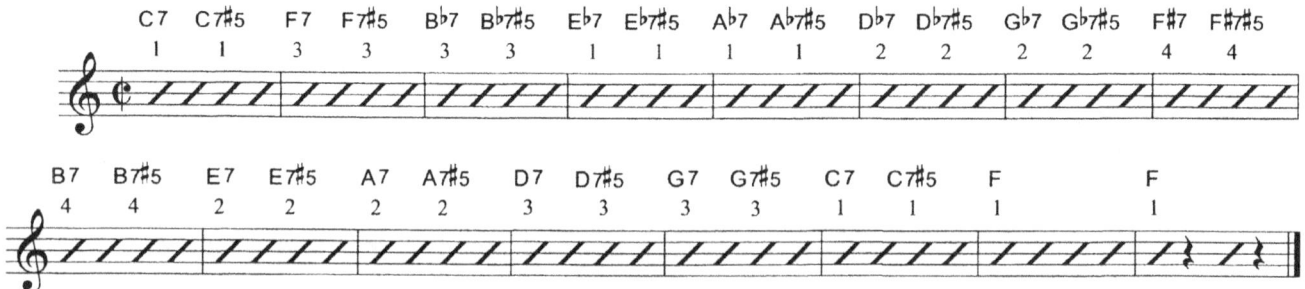

Etude Nine

Mel Bay

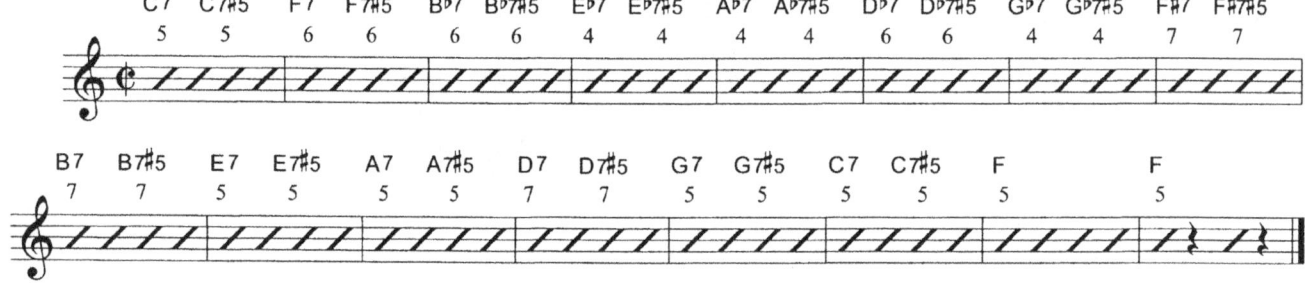

The Major Seventh Chord
Symbol (Ma7)

The major seventh chord is made by raising the 7th tone of the dominant 7th chord a half step, or one fret.

The "**X**" in the Ma7 forms shows the position of the 7th tone (◆) before raising.

Because of the 1/2 tone dissonance between the root and raised 7th, the form $\boxed{I^7}$ is omitted.

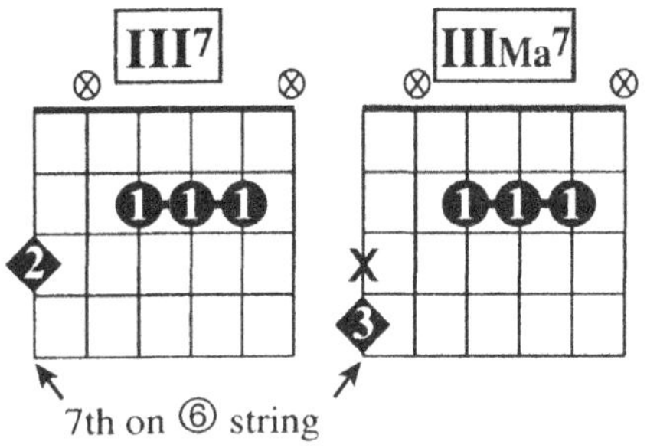

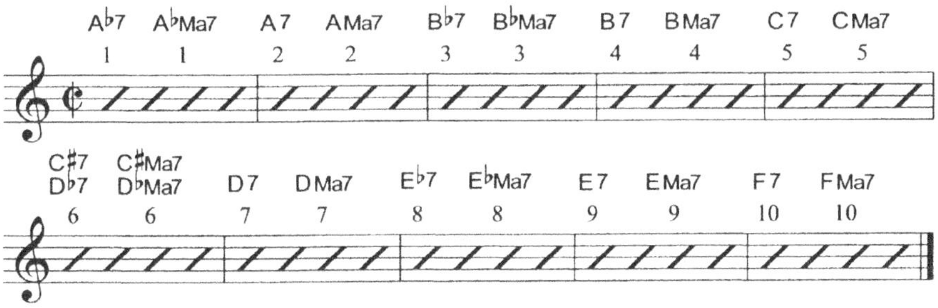

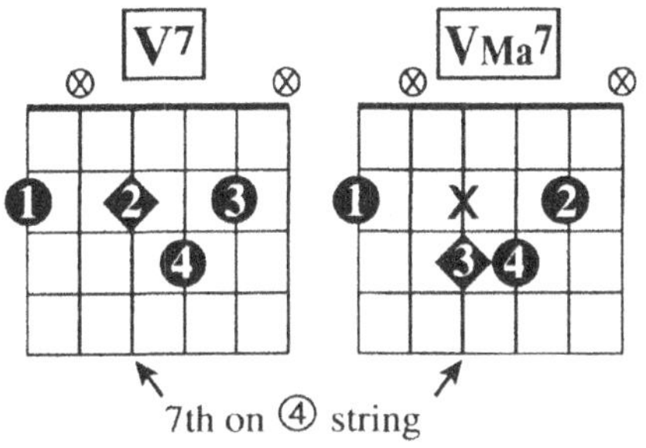

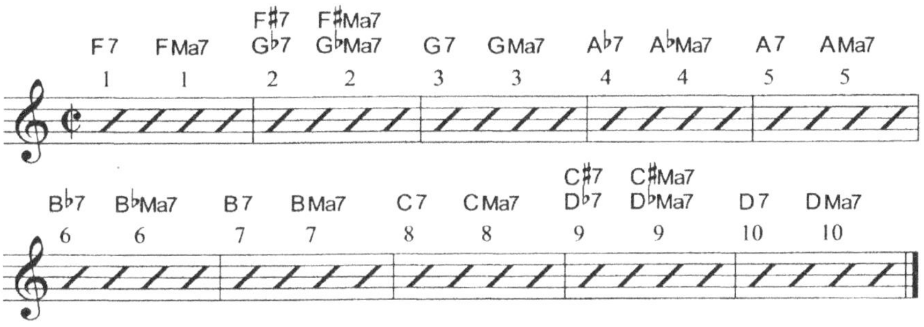

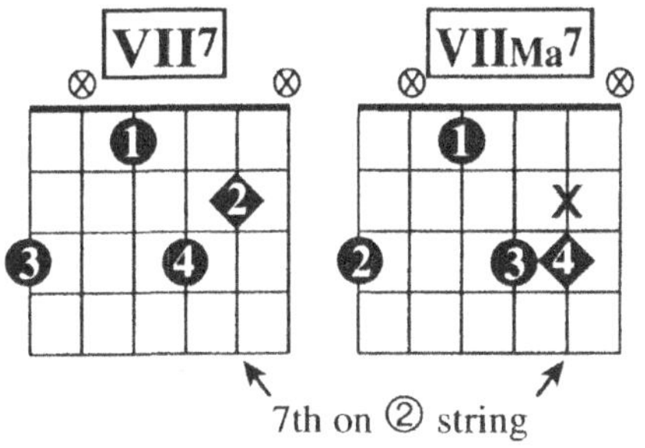

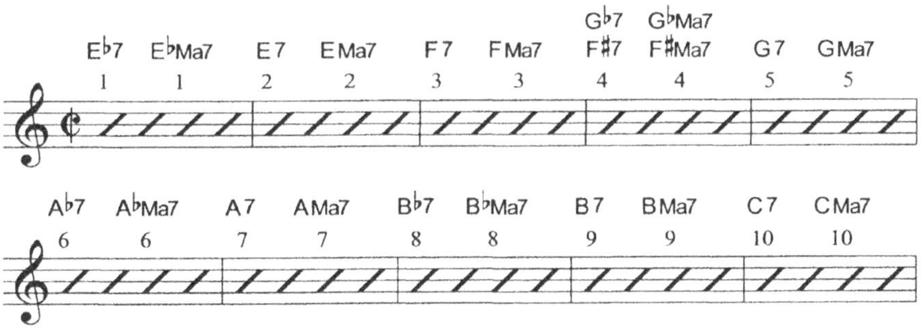

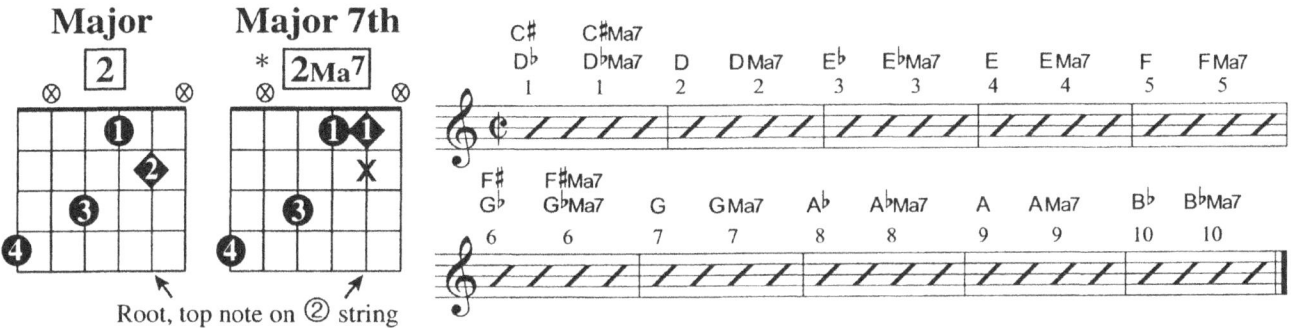

Another Very Useful Ma7 Form

It is made by lowering the root (◆), top note of the major form $\boxed{2}$.

* Note: The $\boxed{2Ma^7}$ form contains only the tones of a pure minor chord, but due to it's effectiveness as major 7th harmony, it is included as a Ma7 form.

Exercise Employing Forms II_{Ma^7} and V_{Ma^7}

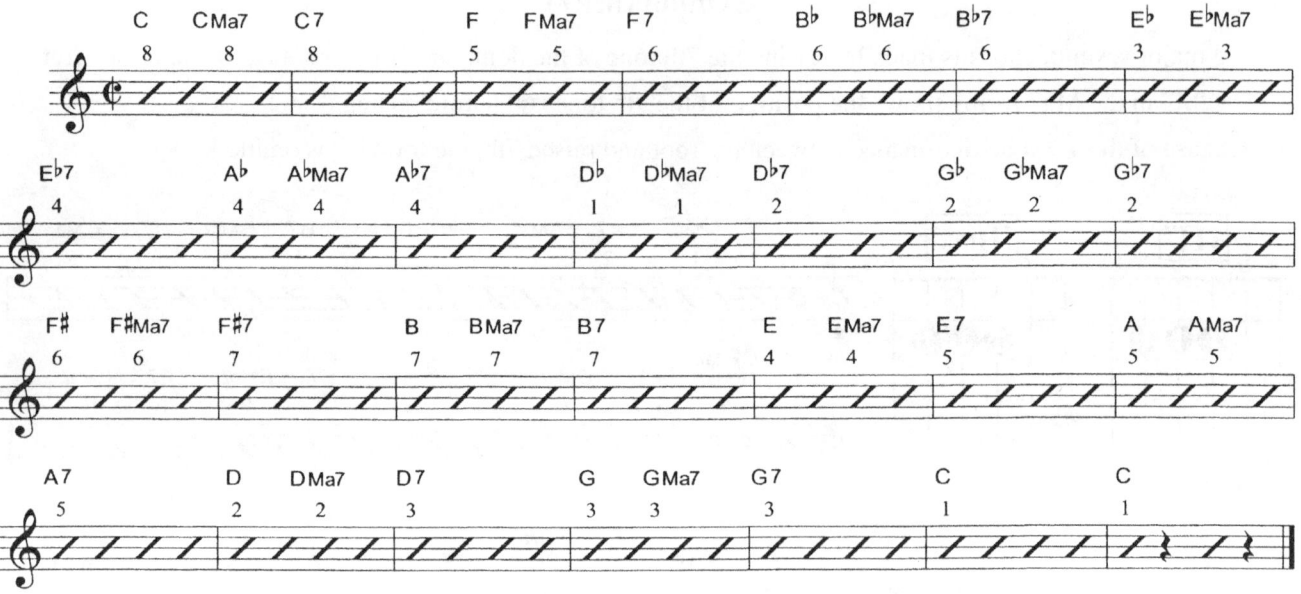

Exercise Employing Forms III_{Ma^7} and VII_{Ma^7}

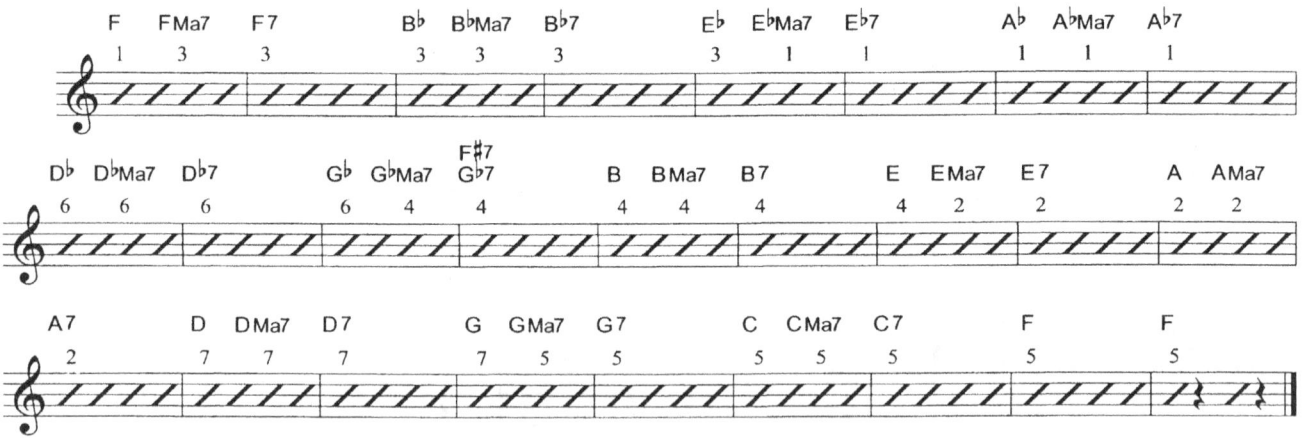

Etude Ten

Mel Bay

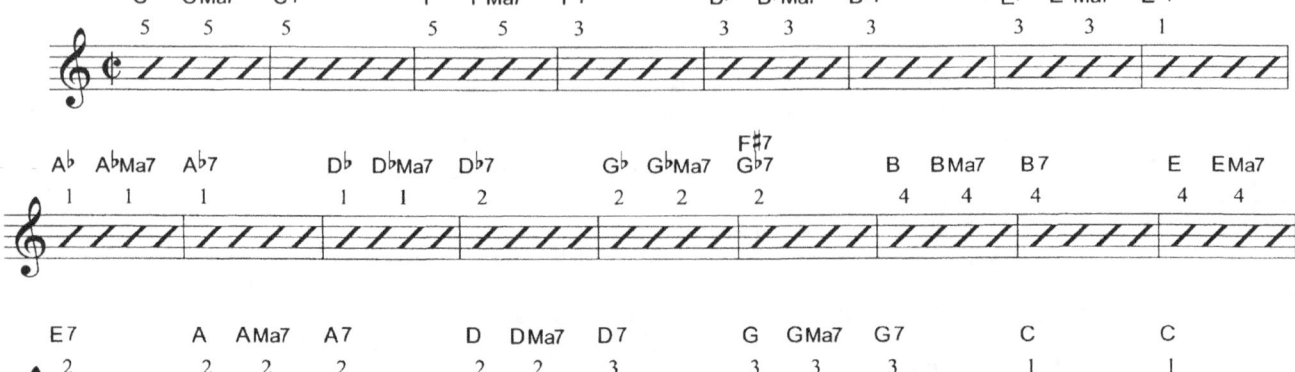

The Major Sixth Chords

Symbol (6) = Major sixth

By lowering the seventh tone of the dominant 7th chord one fret, it becomes the sixth tone, thus forming the major sixth chord.

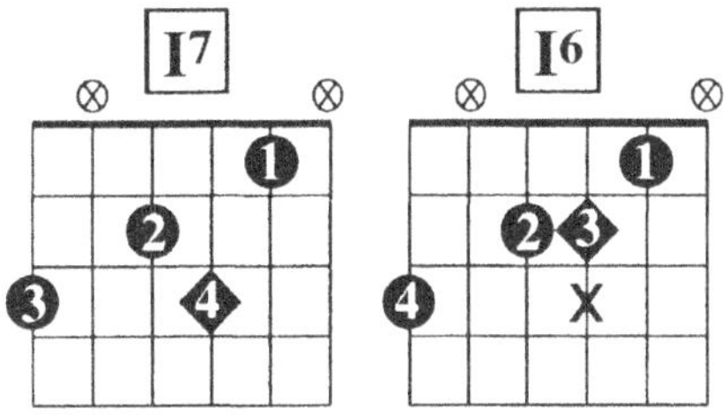

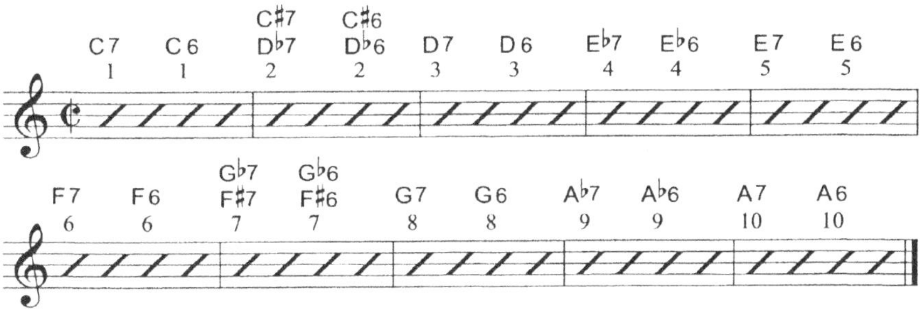

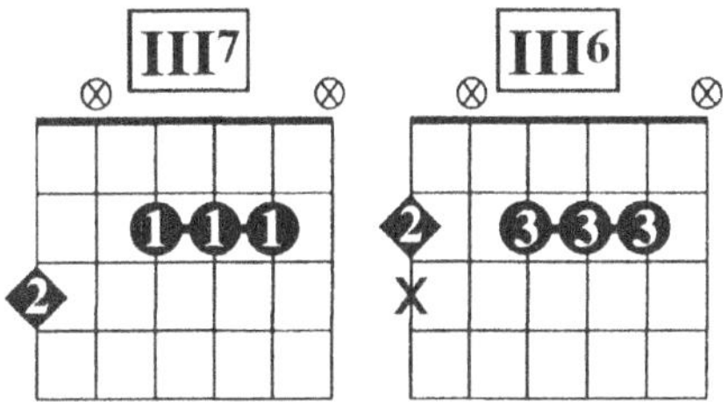

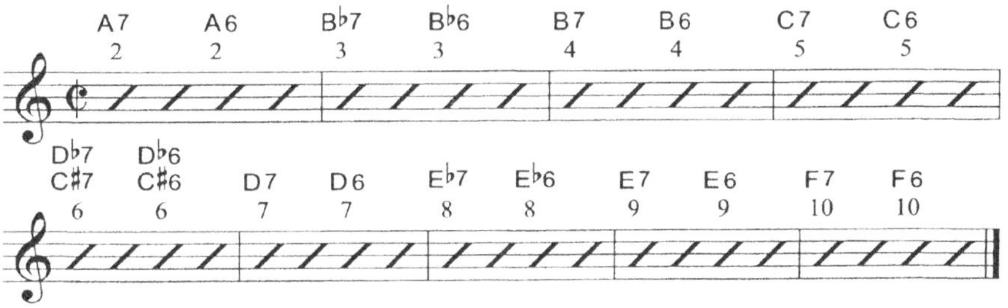

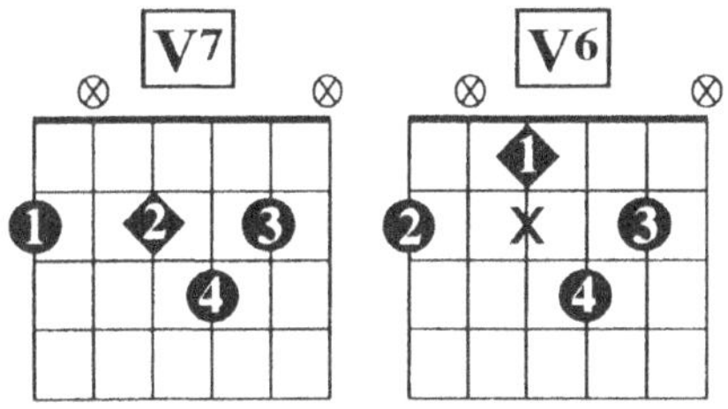

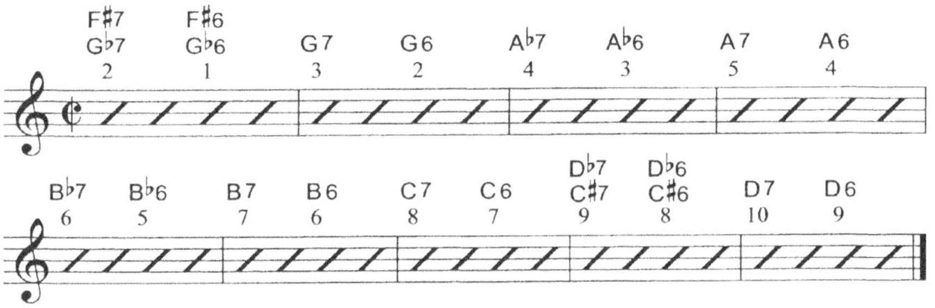

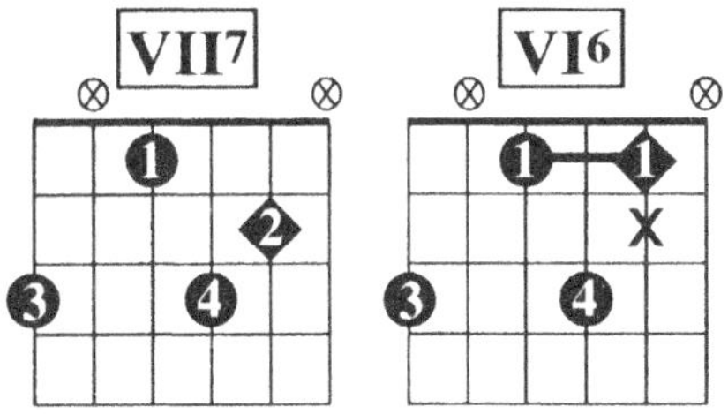

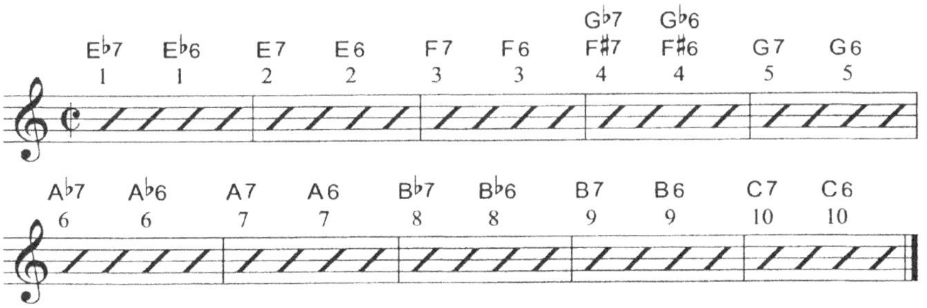

Top note is the 6th tone hence the chord is designated as form six, thus VI⁶

Exercise Employing Forms I⁶ and V⁶

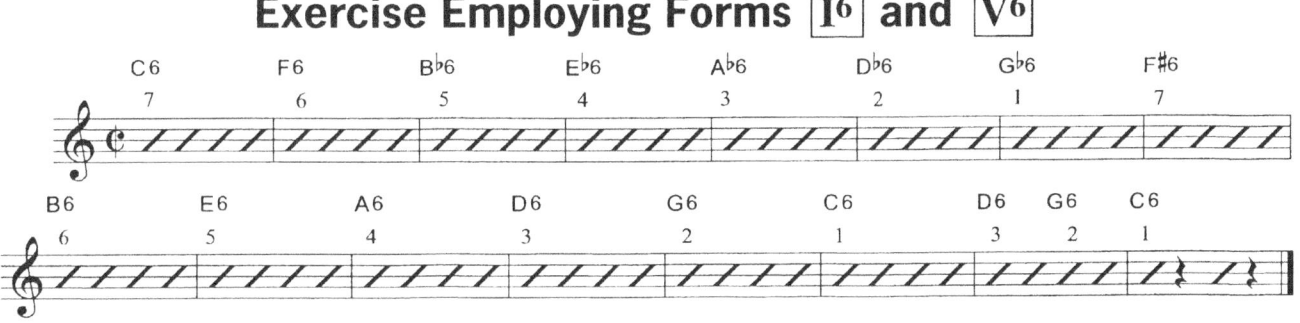

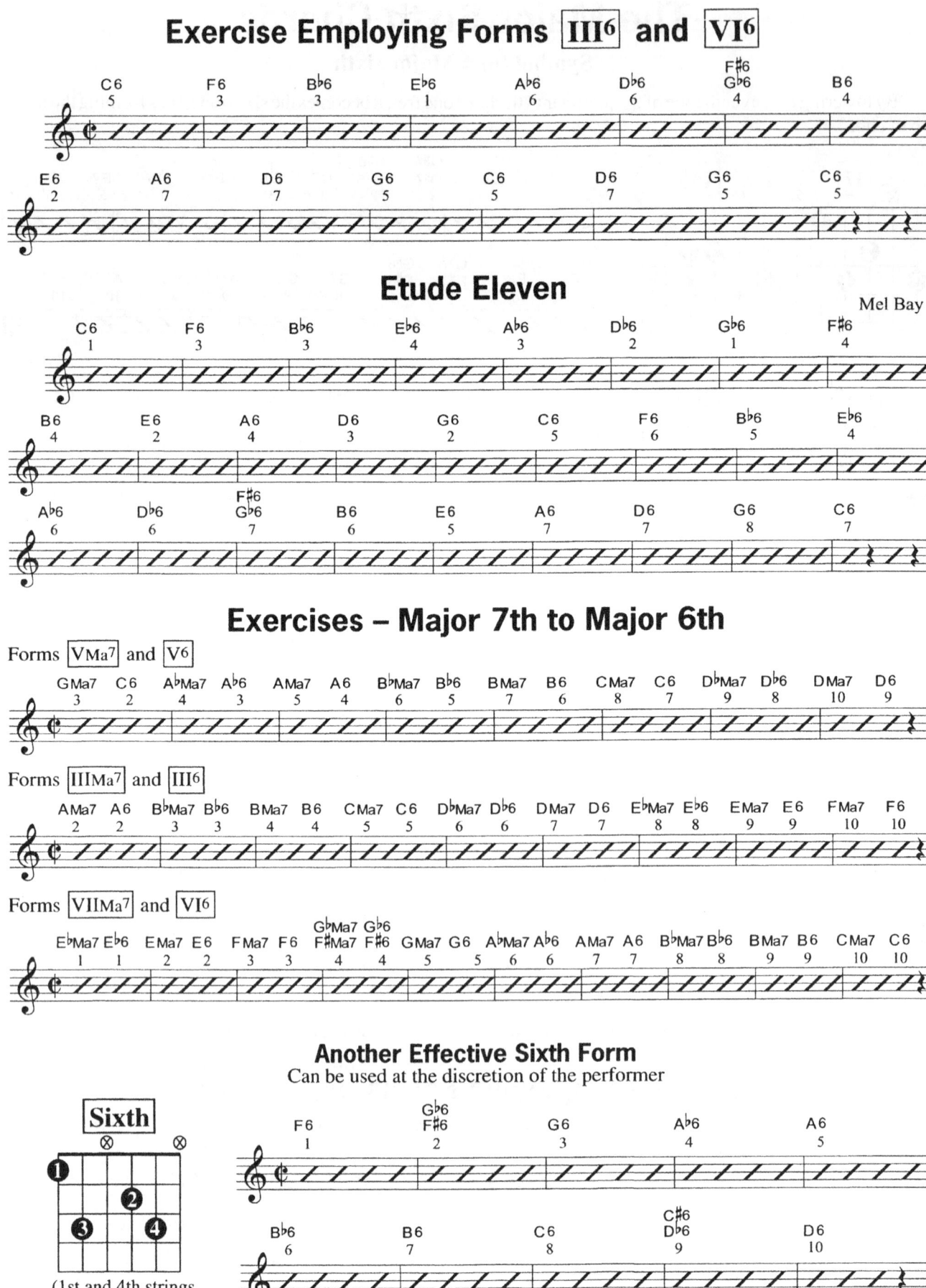

The Minor Sixth Chord

Symbol (m6) = minor sixth

This chord is made by lowering the 3rd of the major sixth chord one fret.

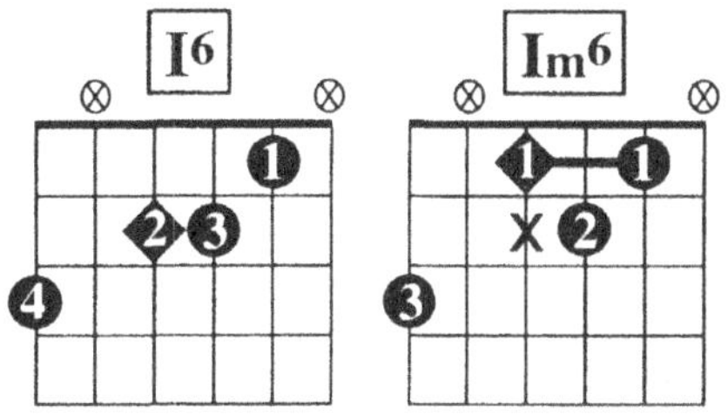

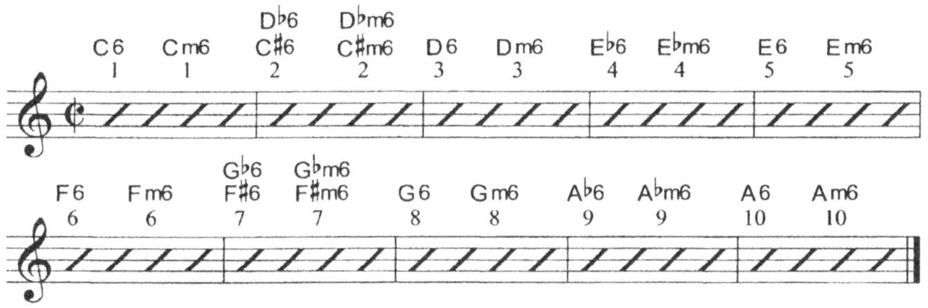

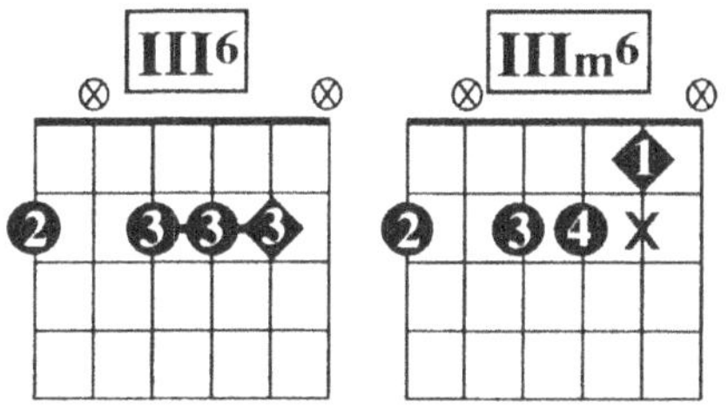

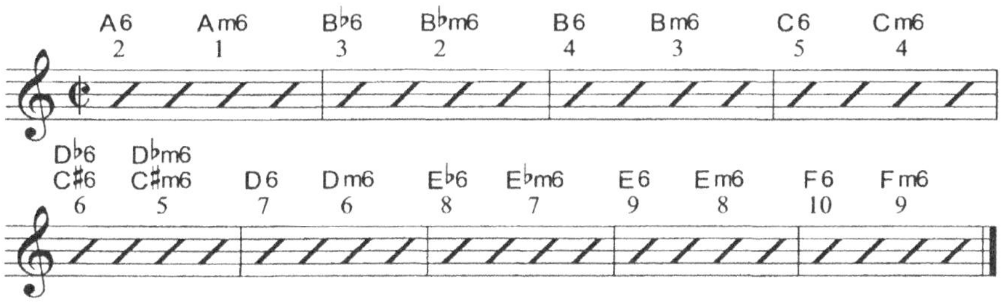

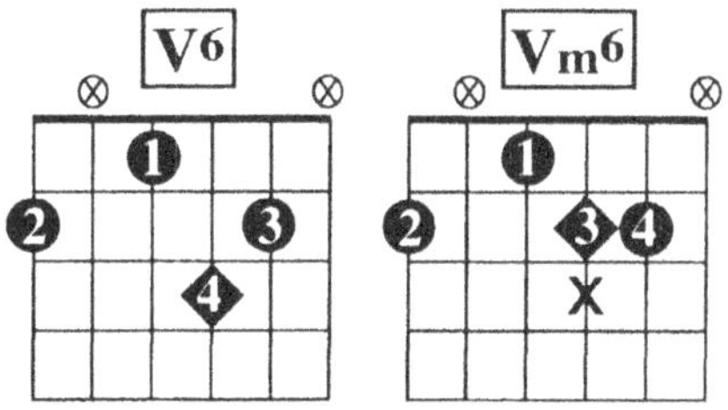

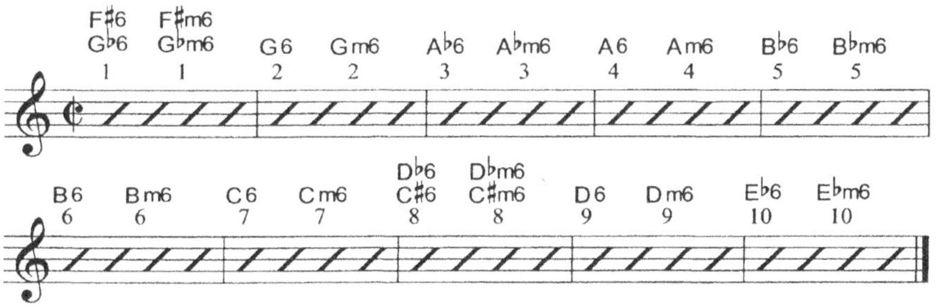

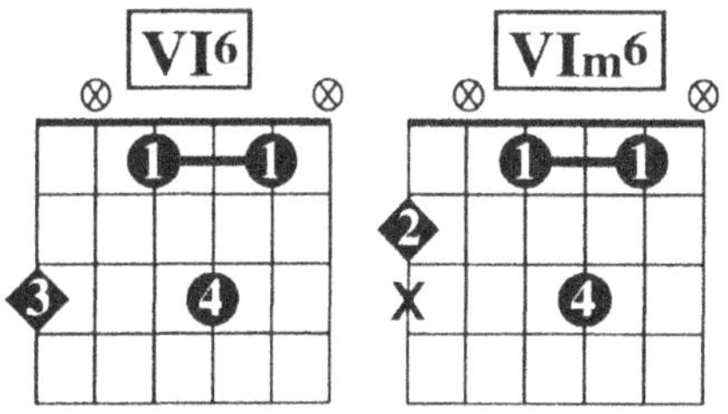

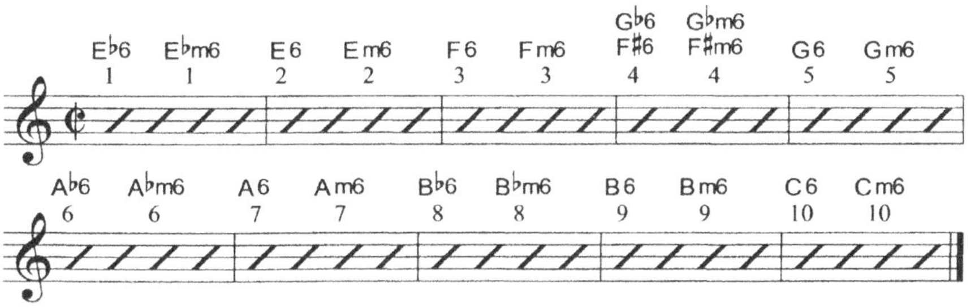

Exercise – Major 6th to Minor 6th

Employing forms I and V

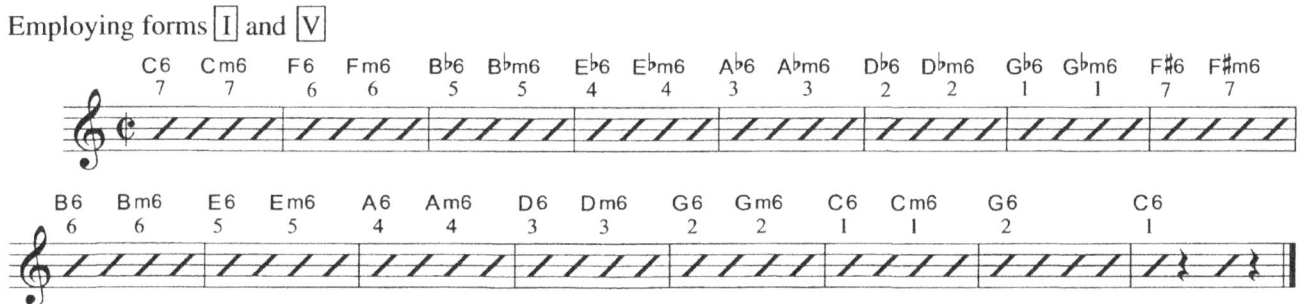

The Diminished Chord

Symbol (°). Sometimes (–) and (dim) are used.

The chord is made by lowering the 3rd, 5th and 7th of the dominant 7th chord.

Only the root remains in position.

The three movable tones are indicated by the diamond (◆).

The "**X**" marks in the diminished forms show the original position of the 3rd, 5th and 7th.

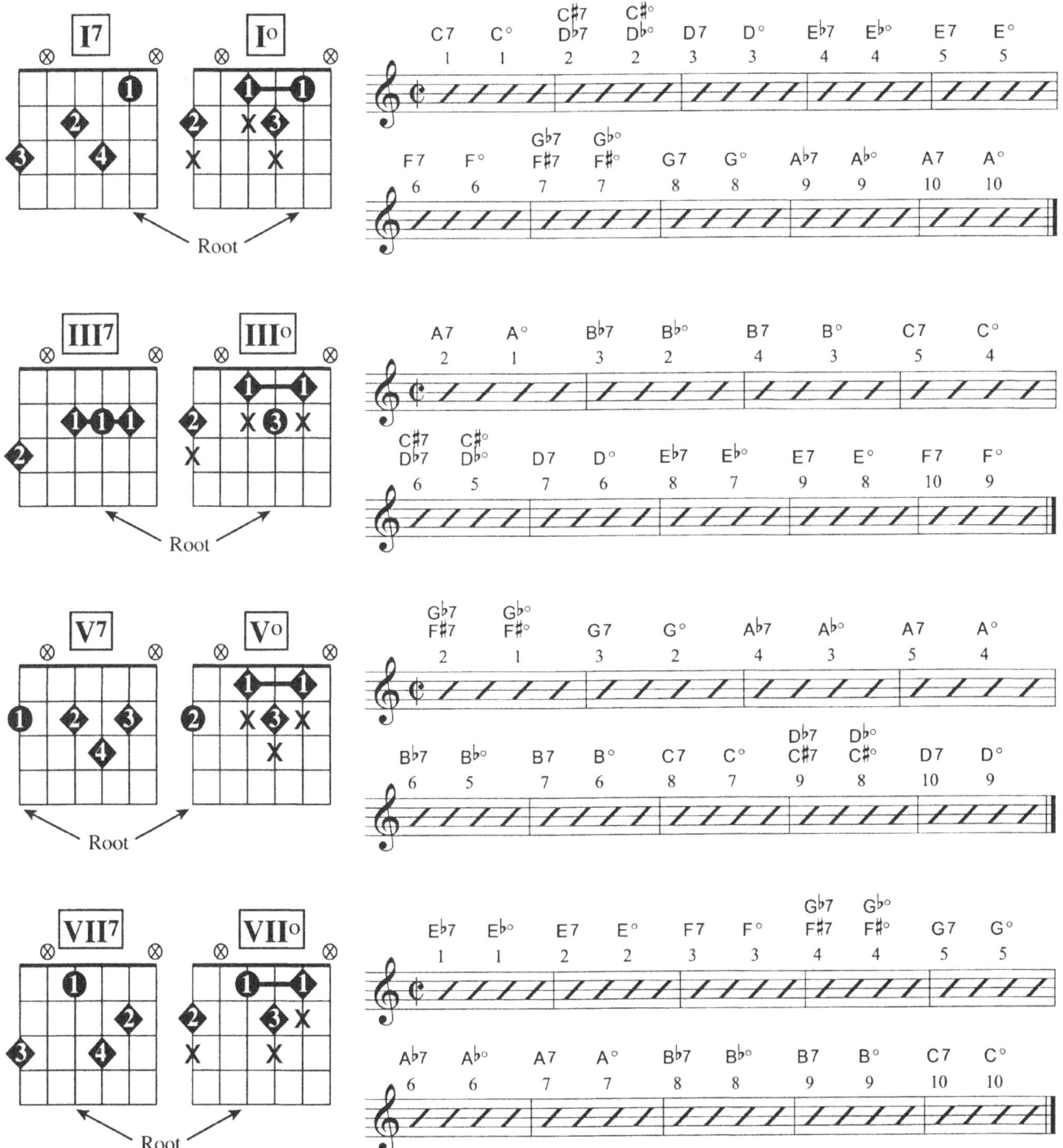

The Augmented Chord

Only one form is necessary. The chord is indicated by the symbol (+). Sometimes the abbreviation *Aug* is used. The inversions are produced at the various frets by using only this one form.

Inversions

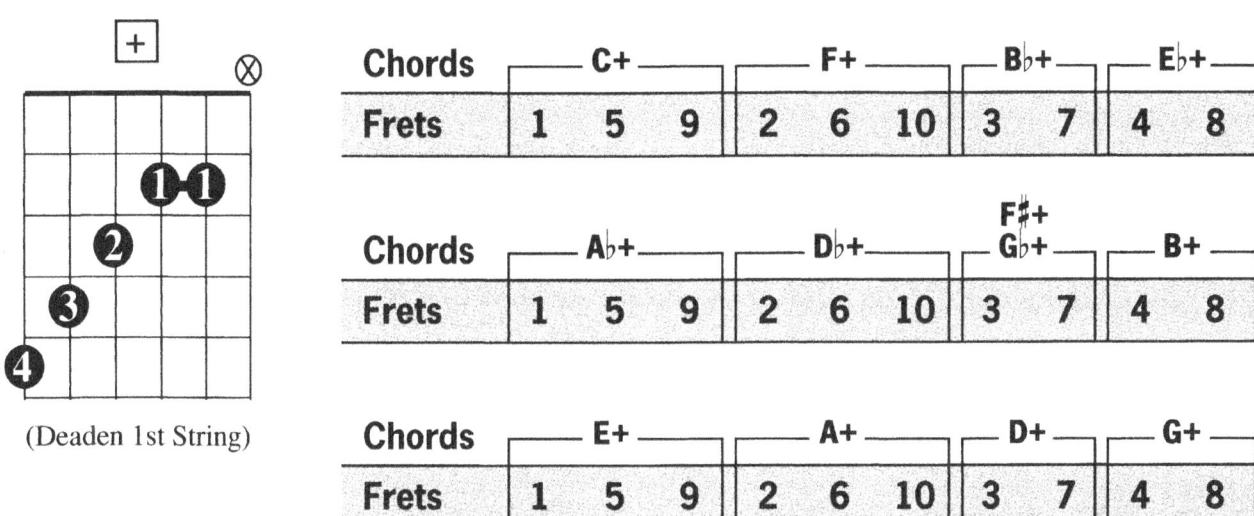

(Deaden 1st String)

Augmented Stuff

Mel Bay

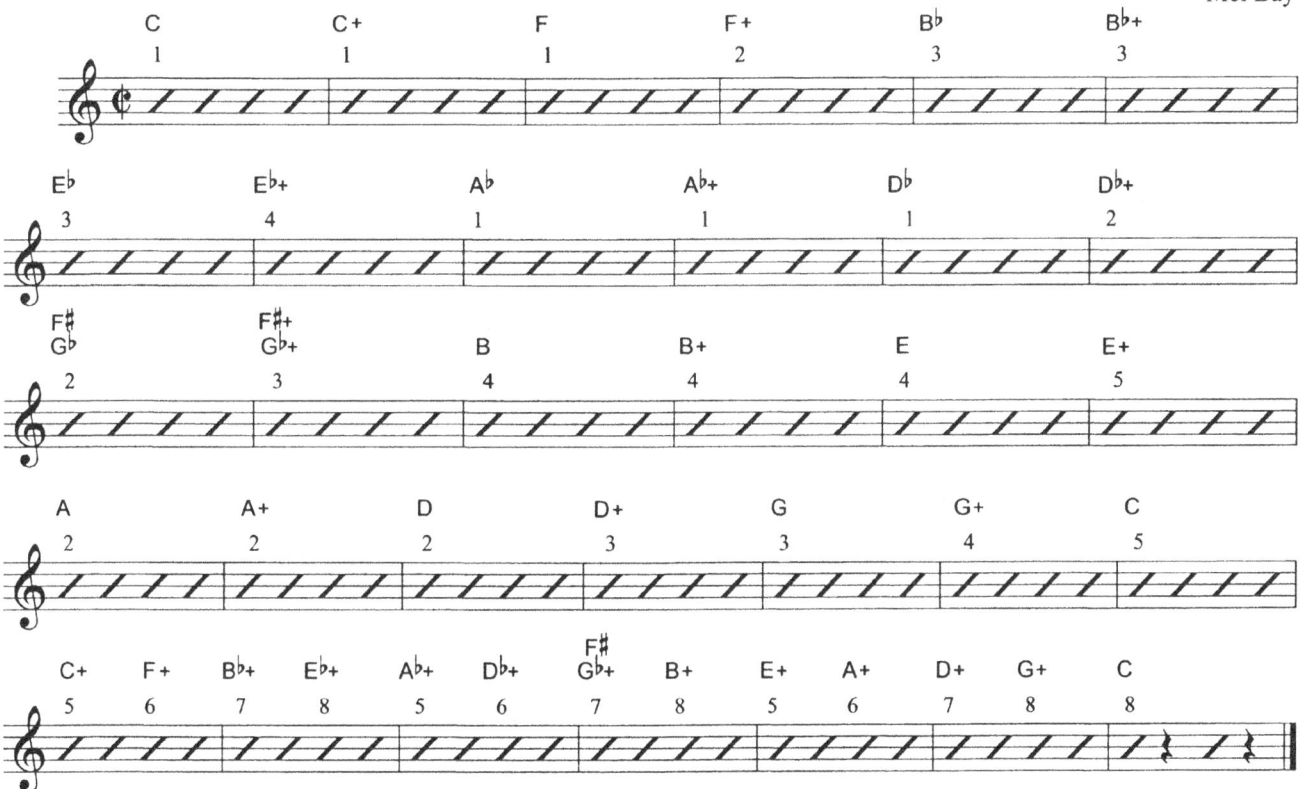

The Ninth Chord

Symbol (9) = Ninth chord

The ninth chord is made by raising the root of the dominant 7th chord a whole tone, or two frets.

The diamond (◆) represents the movable tone.

The "X" in the ninth form shows position of tone before raising.

The 1st and 5th strings are readened. All six strings are strummed.

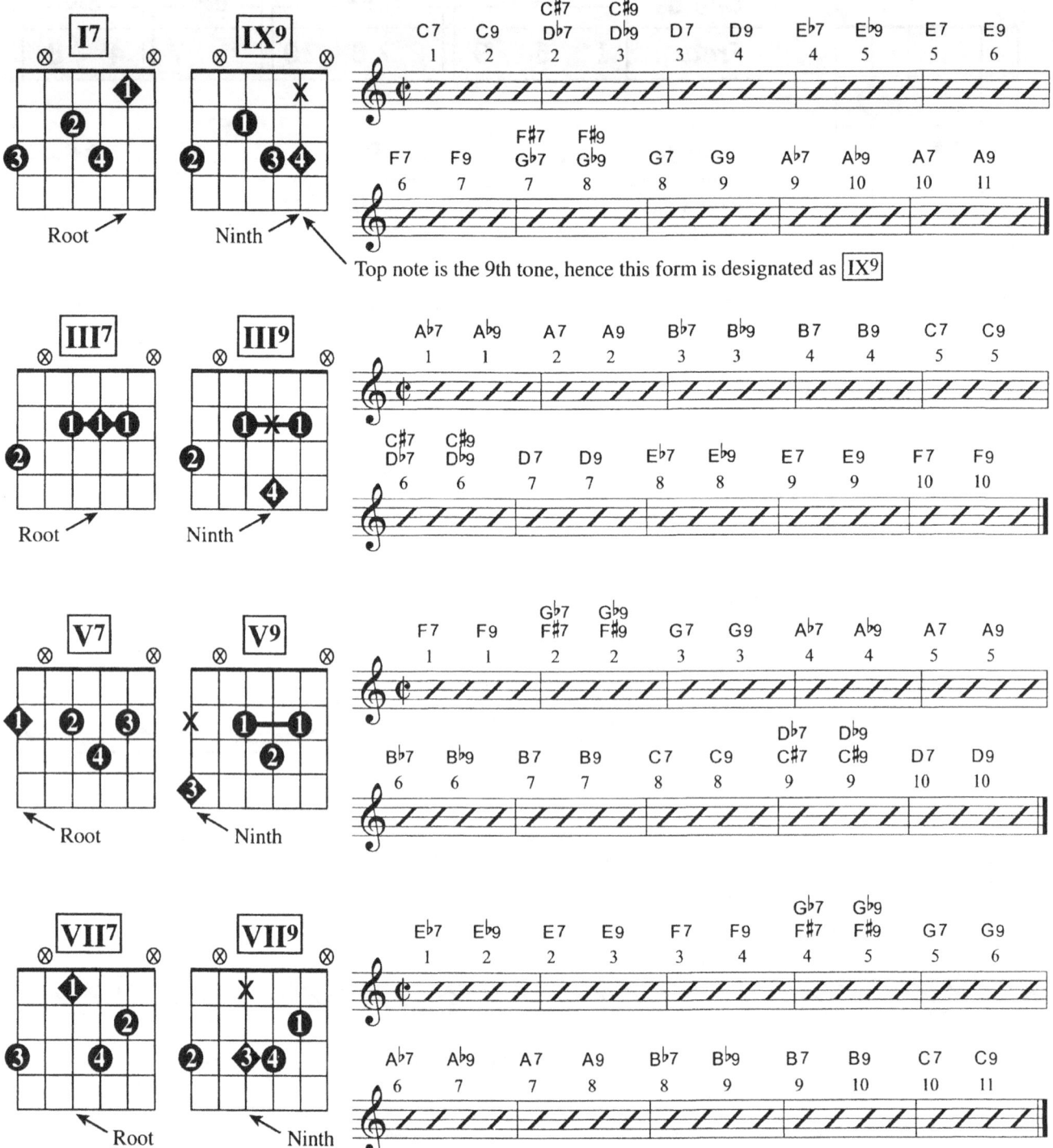

Exercises – Seventh to Ninth

No. 1

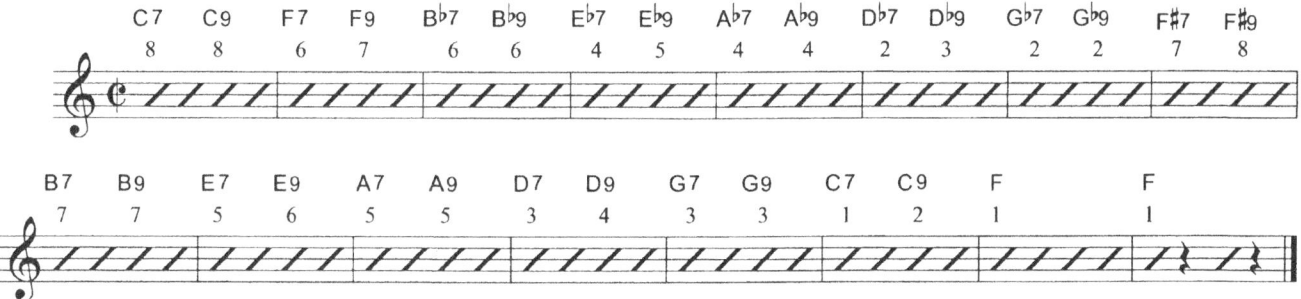

No. 2

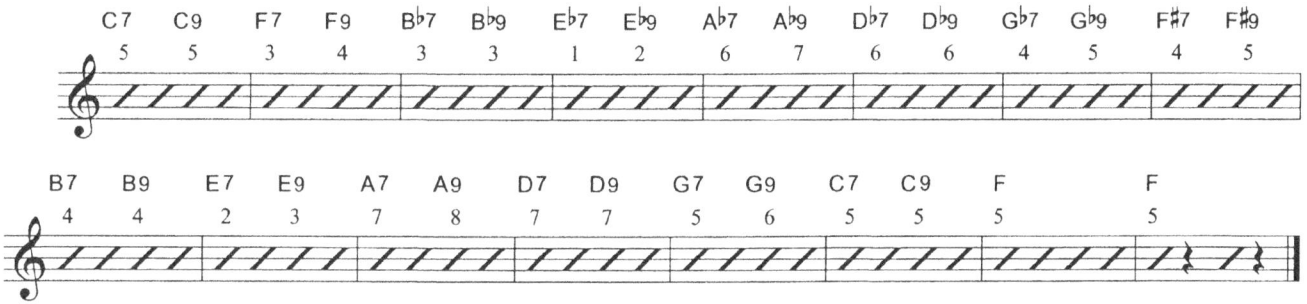

No. 3

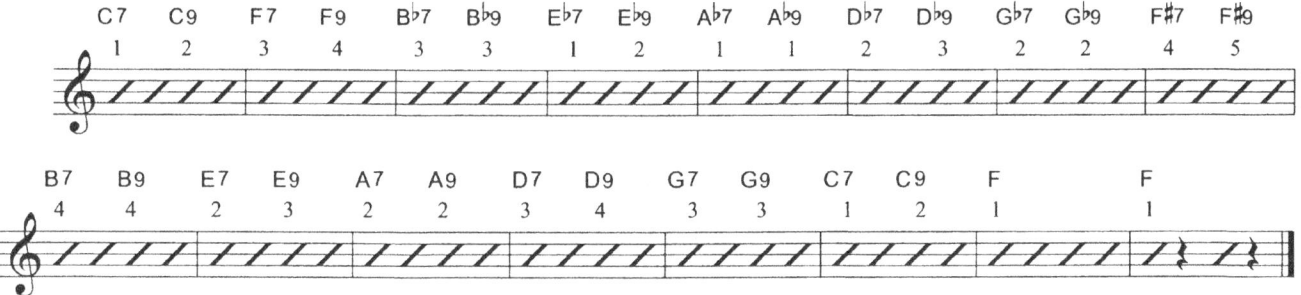

No. 4

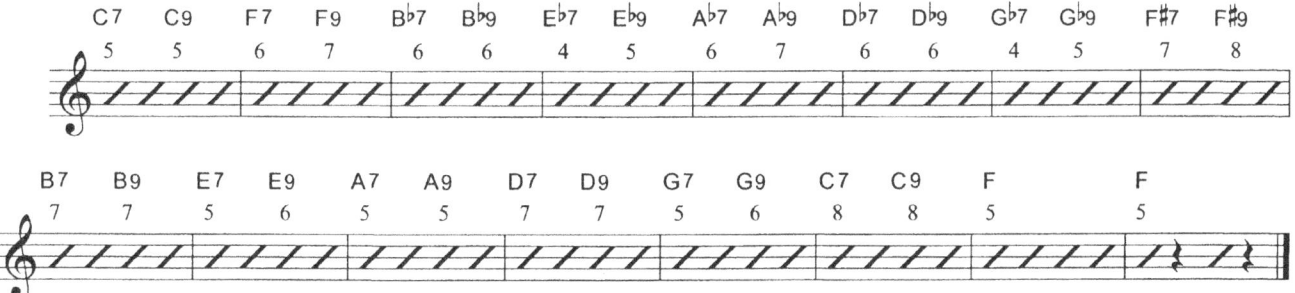

The Minor Ninth Chord

Symbol (m9) = Minor ninth

Lowering the 3rd of the ninth chord a half step, or one fret, produces the minor ninth

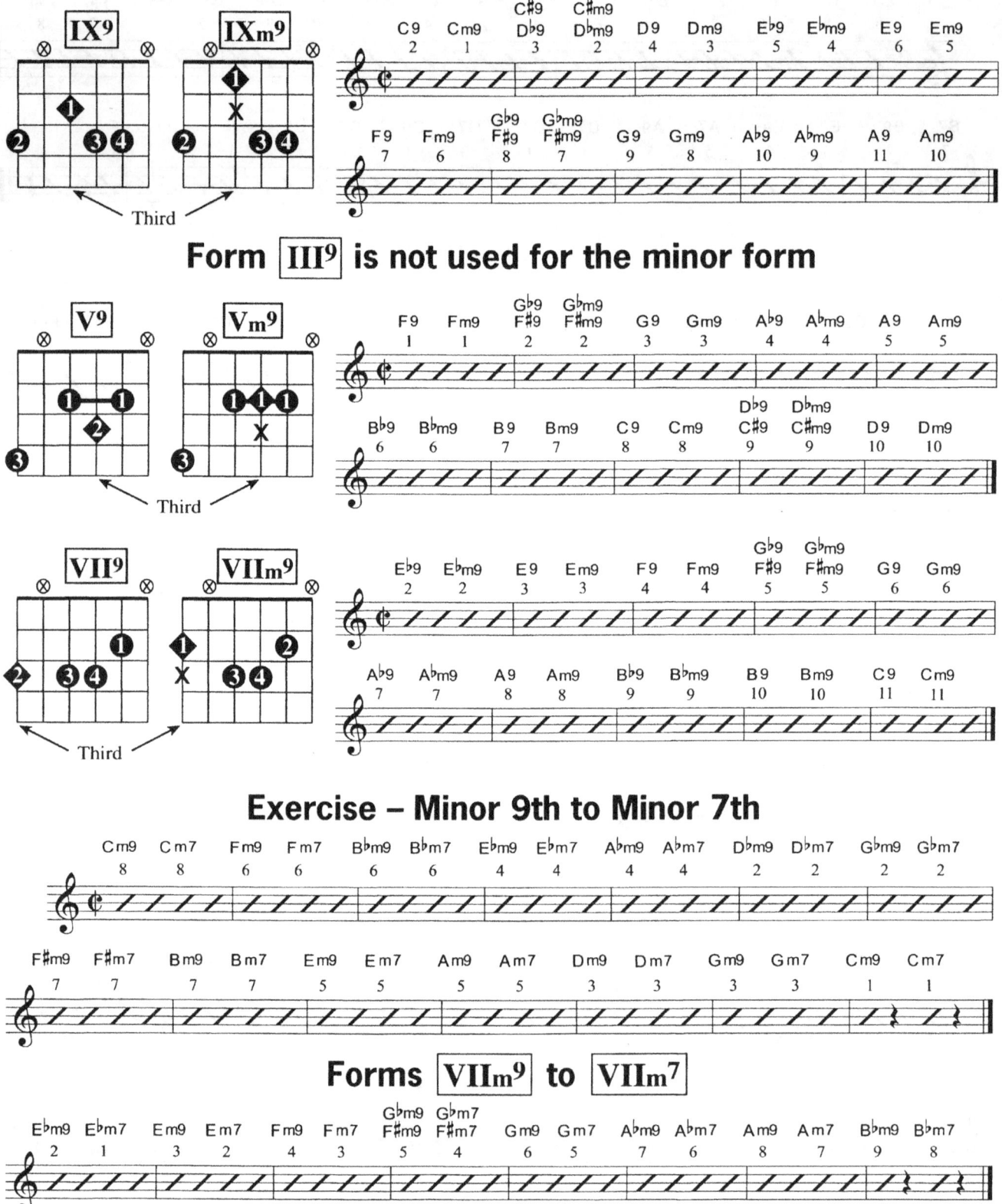

The 9♯5 Chord

Symbol (9♯5) = Nine sharp five chord

This chord is made by raising the 5th of the 9th chord one fret, (◆) = fifth.

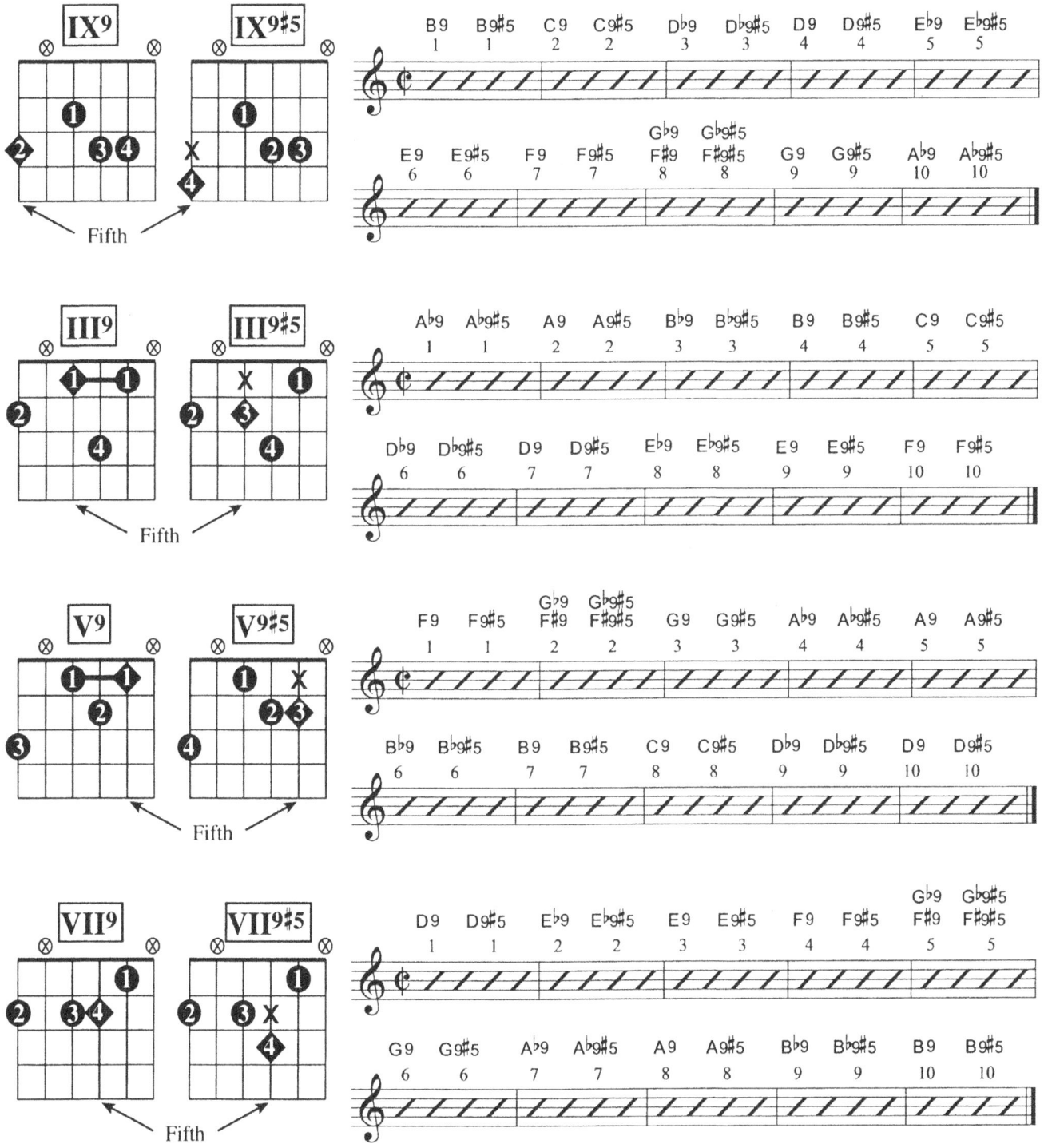

Exercises – 9th to 9♯5

No. 1

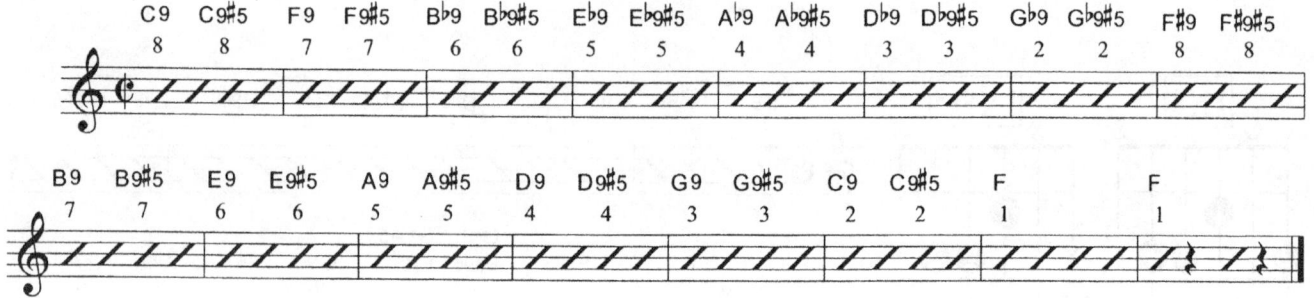

No. 2

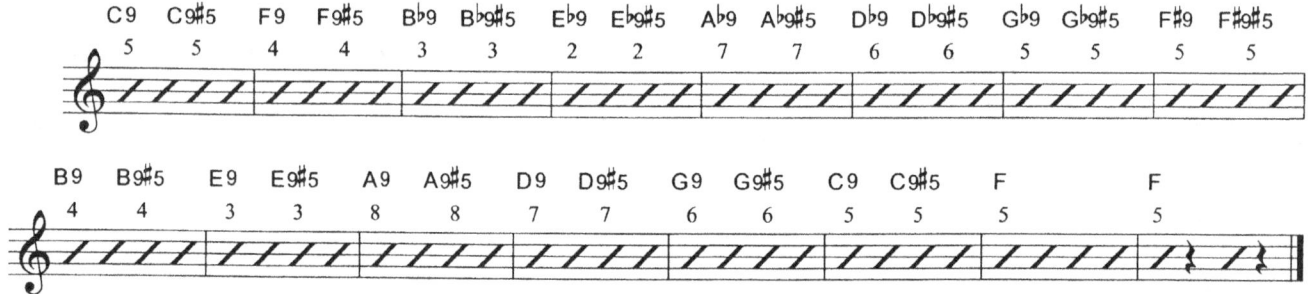

No. 3

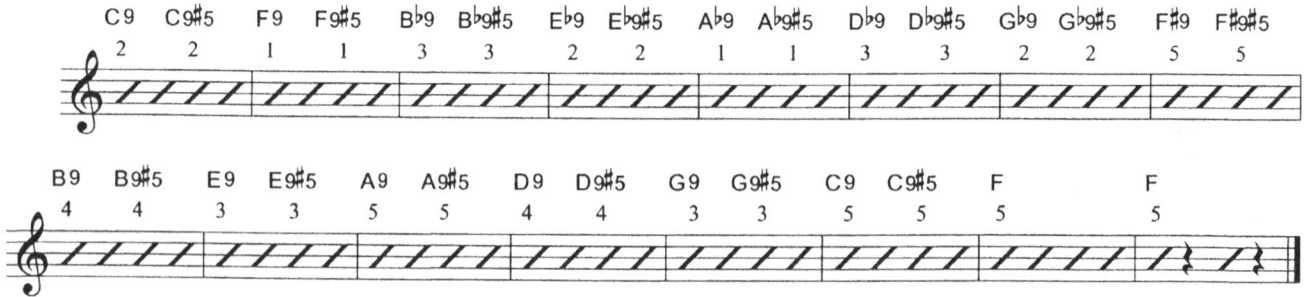

No. 4

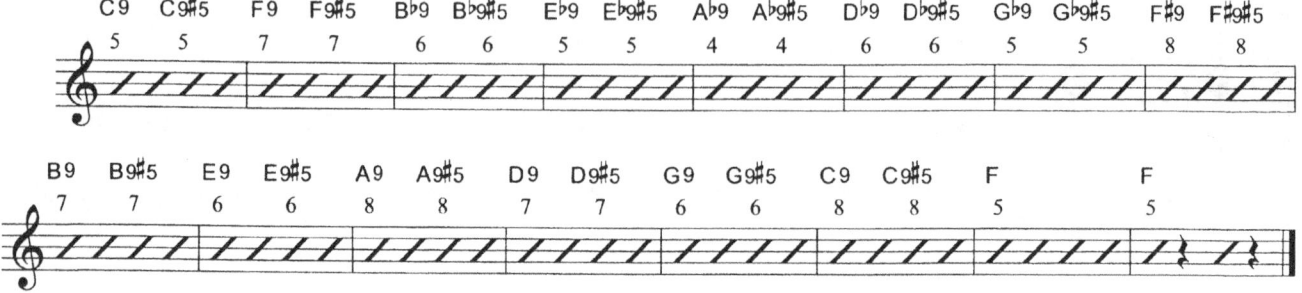

The 9♭5 Chord

Symbol (9♭5) = Nine flat five chord

This chord is made by lowering the 5th of the 9th chord one fret.

The diamond (♦) indicates the 5th.

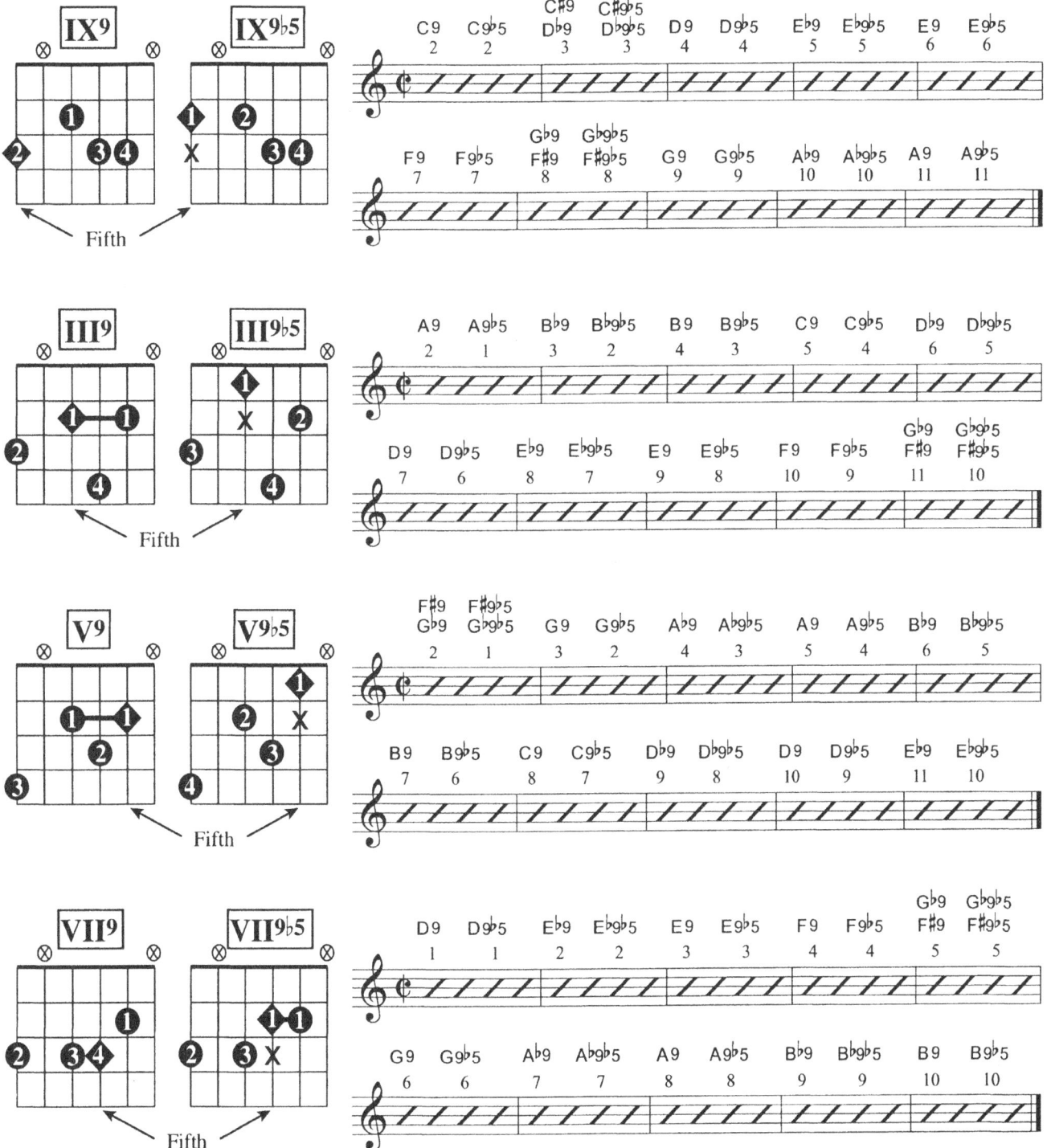

9th to 9♭5 and 7th to 7♯5

No. 1

The Major Ninth Chord

Symbol (Ma9) = Major 9th chord

The major ninth chord is made by raising the 7th (♦) of the 9th chord one fret.

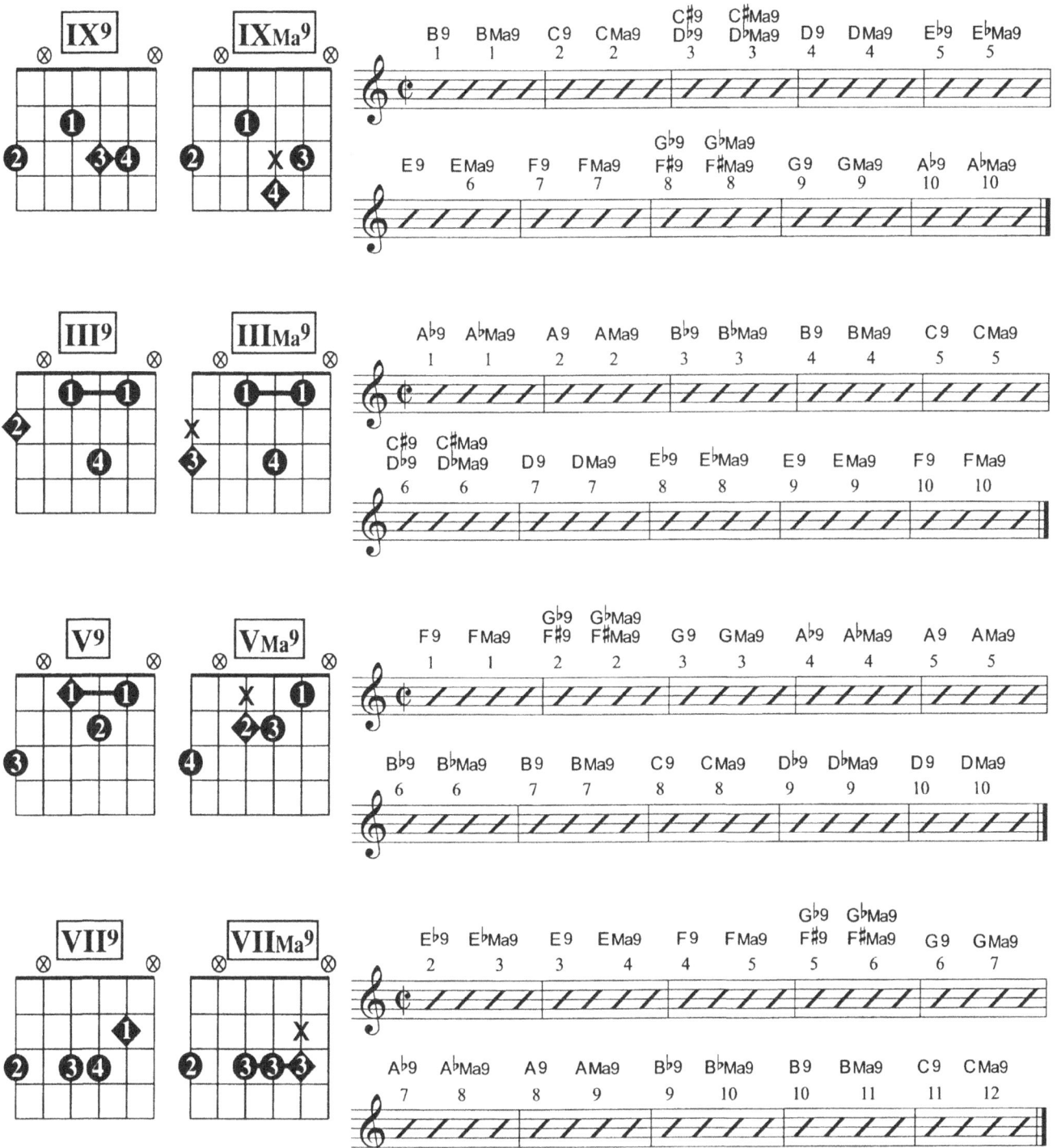

Exercises – Major Ninth to Major Sixth

No. 1

The 7♭9 Chord

Symbol (7♭9) = Seventh flat nine chord

This chord is often designated as 7♭9 or 7-9, it is made by lowering the ninth tone a half step, or one fret. (♦) = 9th tone.

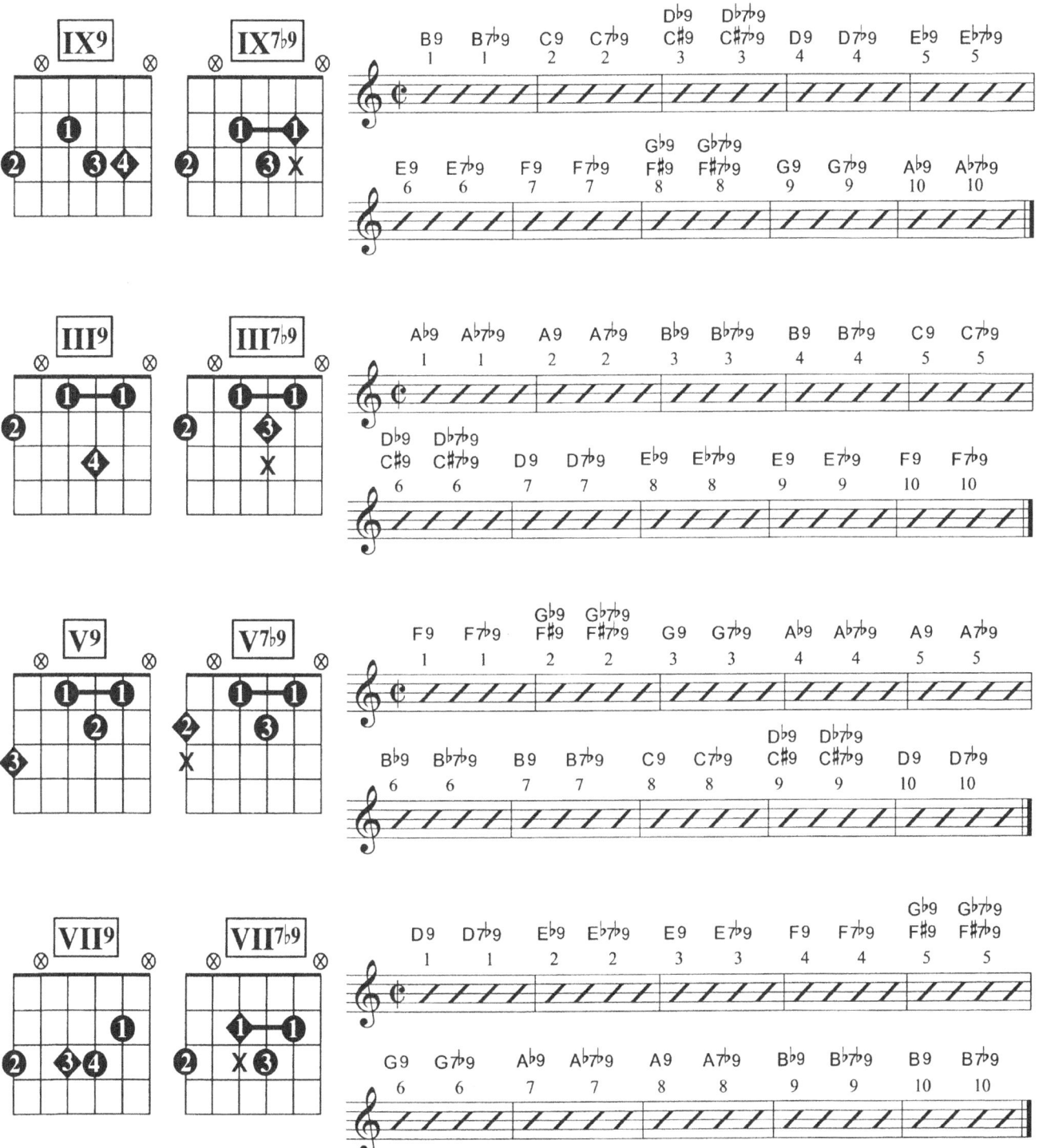

Exercises – Ninth to 7♭9

No. 1

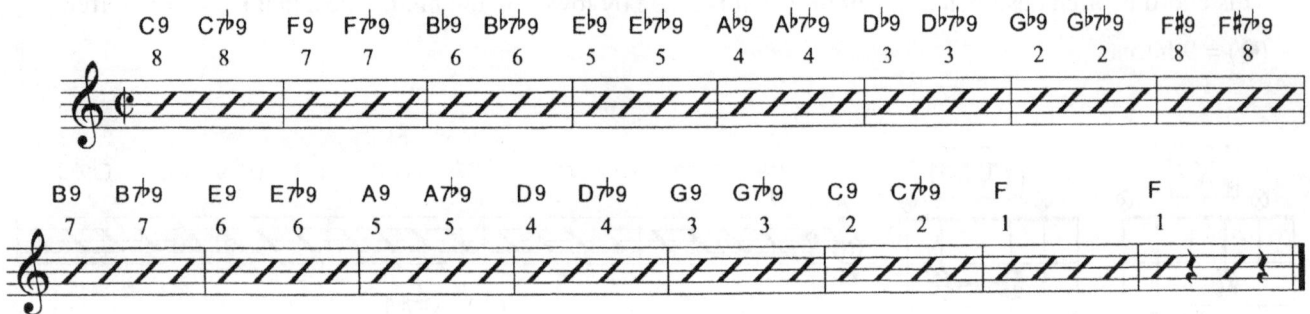

No. 2

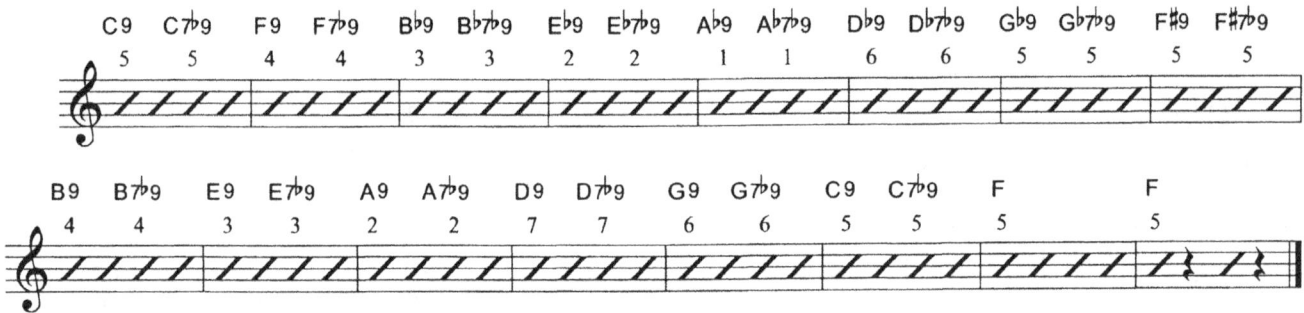

No. 3

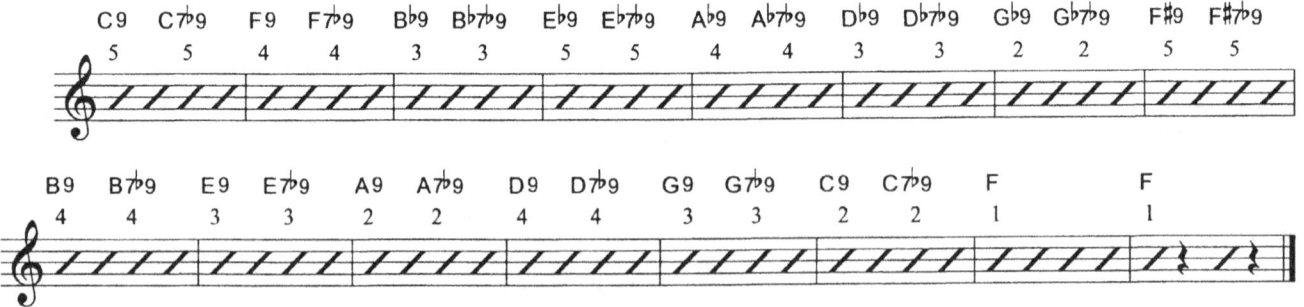

No. 4

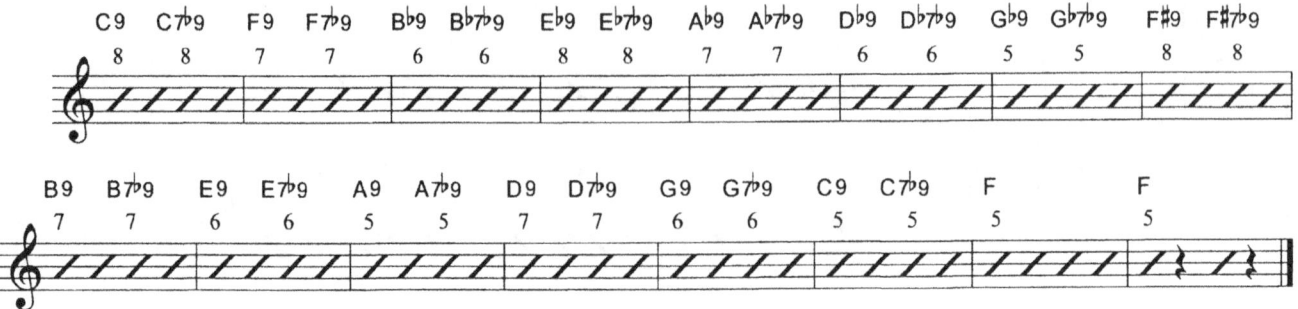

The Augmented Ninth Chord

Symbol (9+) = Augmented 9th chord

The augmented ninth chord is made by raising the 9th (◆) one fret.

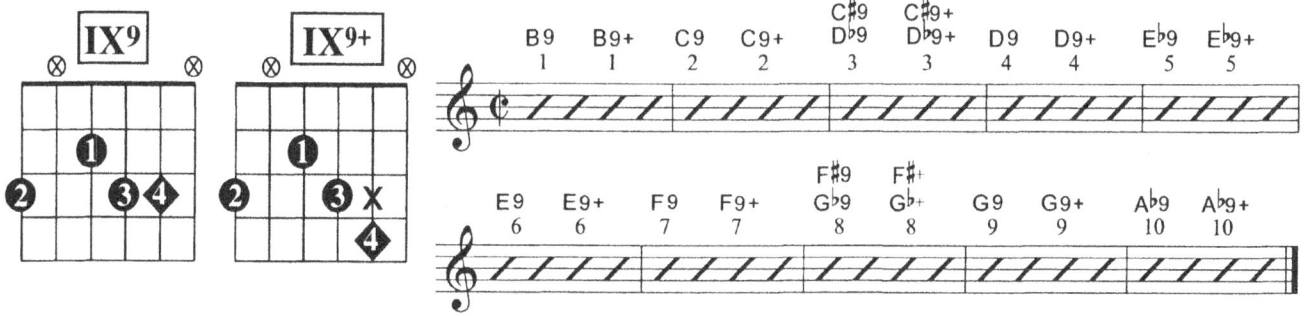

Exercise Using Forms IX^{9+}, $IX^{7\flat9}$, and V^{Ma7}

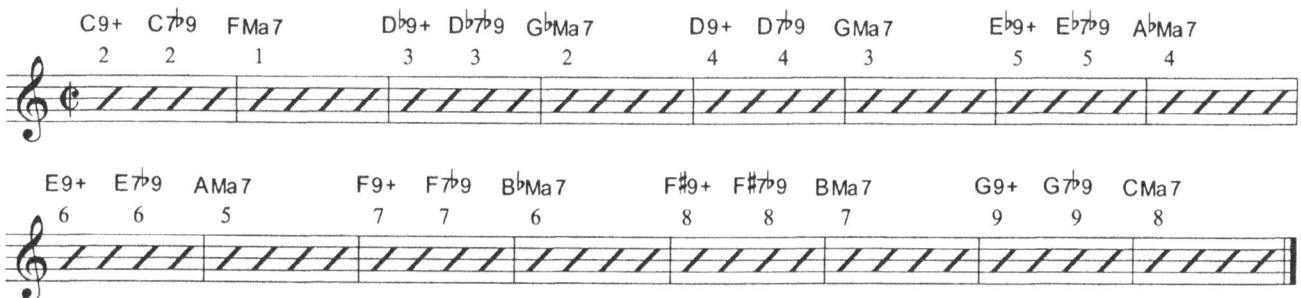

Another Augmented Ninth Form

Designated as form 2^{9+}, this form is more widely used as $13^{\flat9}_{\flat5}$ shown later in this book.
A very effective chord in modern orchestrations. (◆ = 9th, X = position of 9th before raising.)

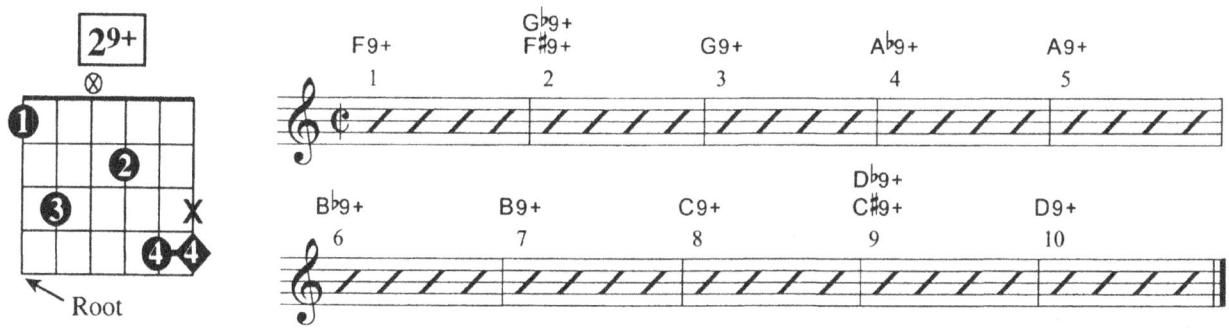

The Eleventh Chord

Symbol (11) = Eleventh chord

By raising the 3rd tone of the ninth chord one fret it becomes the 11th tone, thus producing the eleventh chord.

(♦) = 3rd.

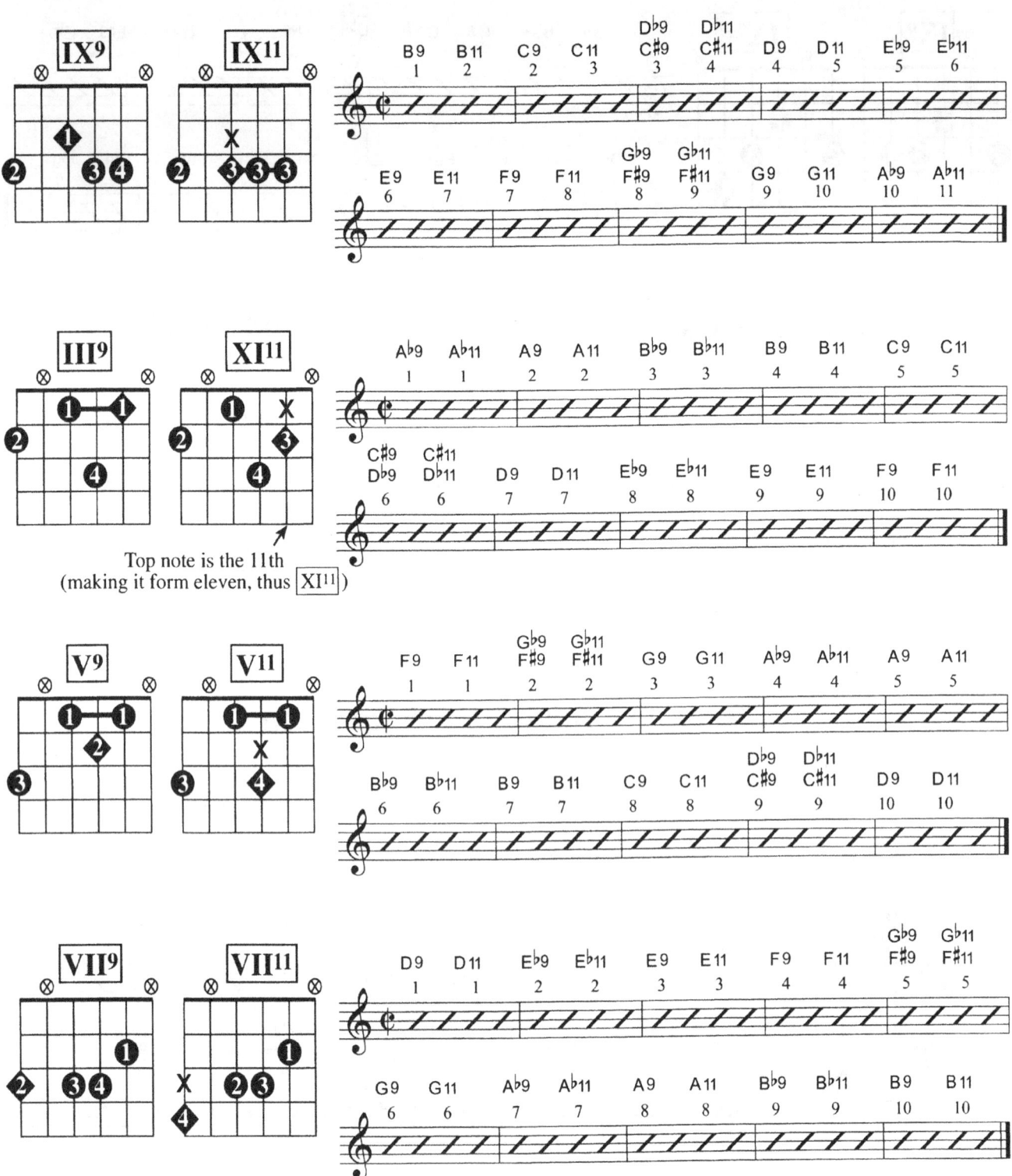

Top note is the 11th (making it form eleven, thus XI¹¹)

Exercise – Eleventh to Ninth

Exercise – Augmented Eleventh

Symbol (11+) = Augmented 11th chord

The augmented 11th chord is made by raising the 11th tone one fret, (◆) = 11th tone.

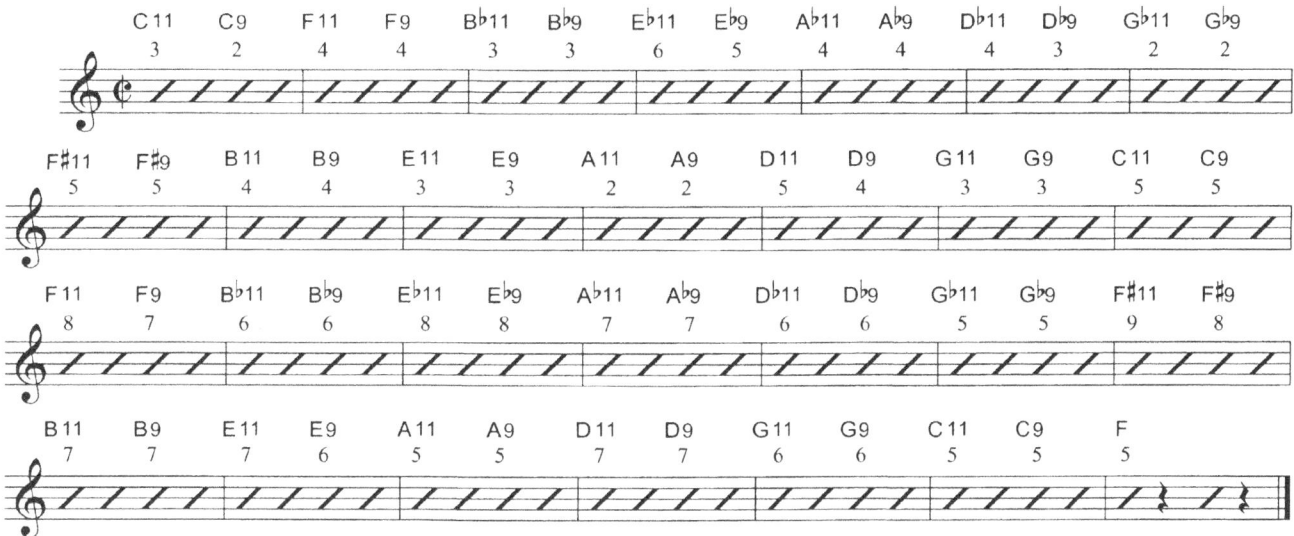

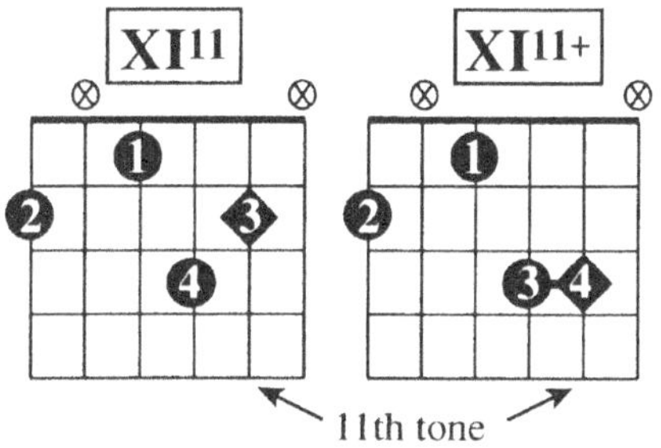

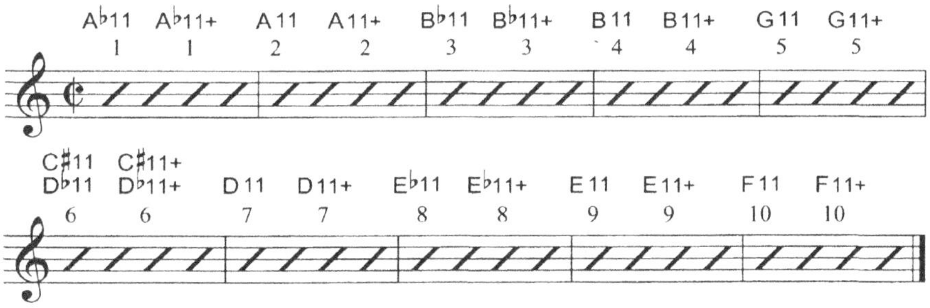

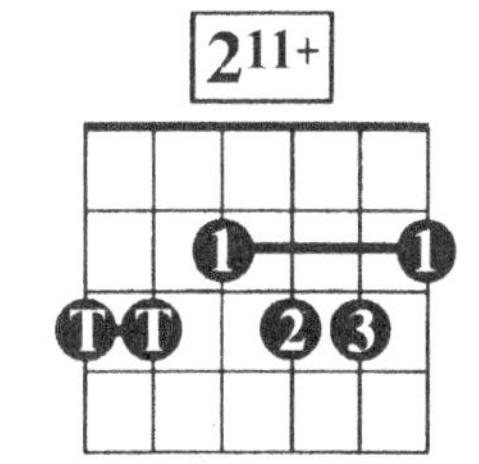

A Six-String Form

Widely used, it is designated as form two, thus 2¹¹⁺

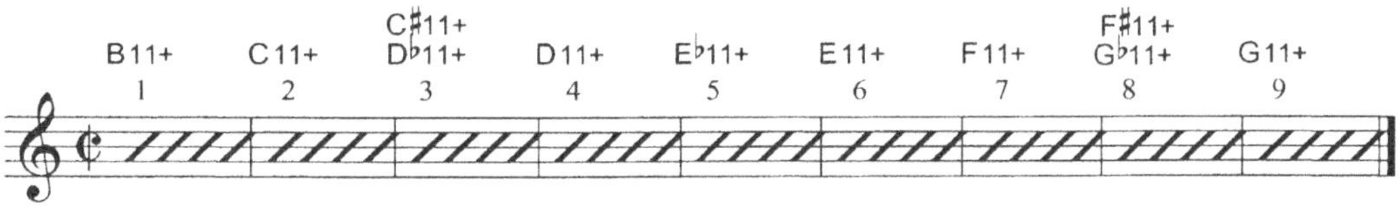

Strings ⑤ and ⑥ are held with the thumb (T = thumb)

Exercise – Employing Forms XI¹¹⁺ and 2¹¹⁺

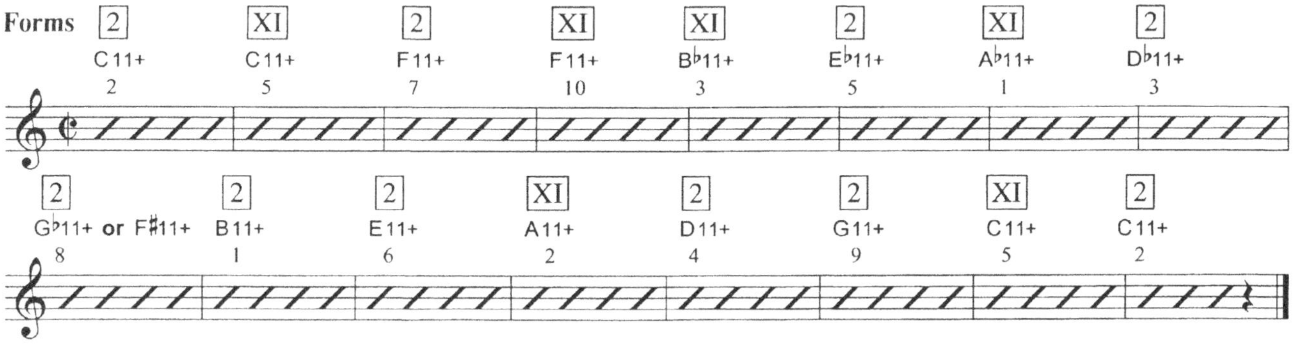

The Thirteenth Chord
Symbol (13) = 13th chord

This great chord is used as a substitute for the 7th or 9th chord in modern orchestral accompaniment. Sometimes it is designated as (7add6) or (9add6).

Four widely used forms are shown. ⊗ = Deadened string

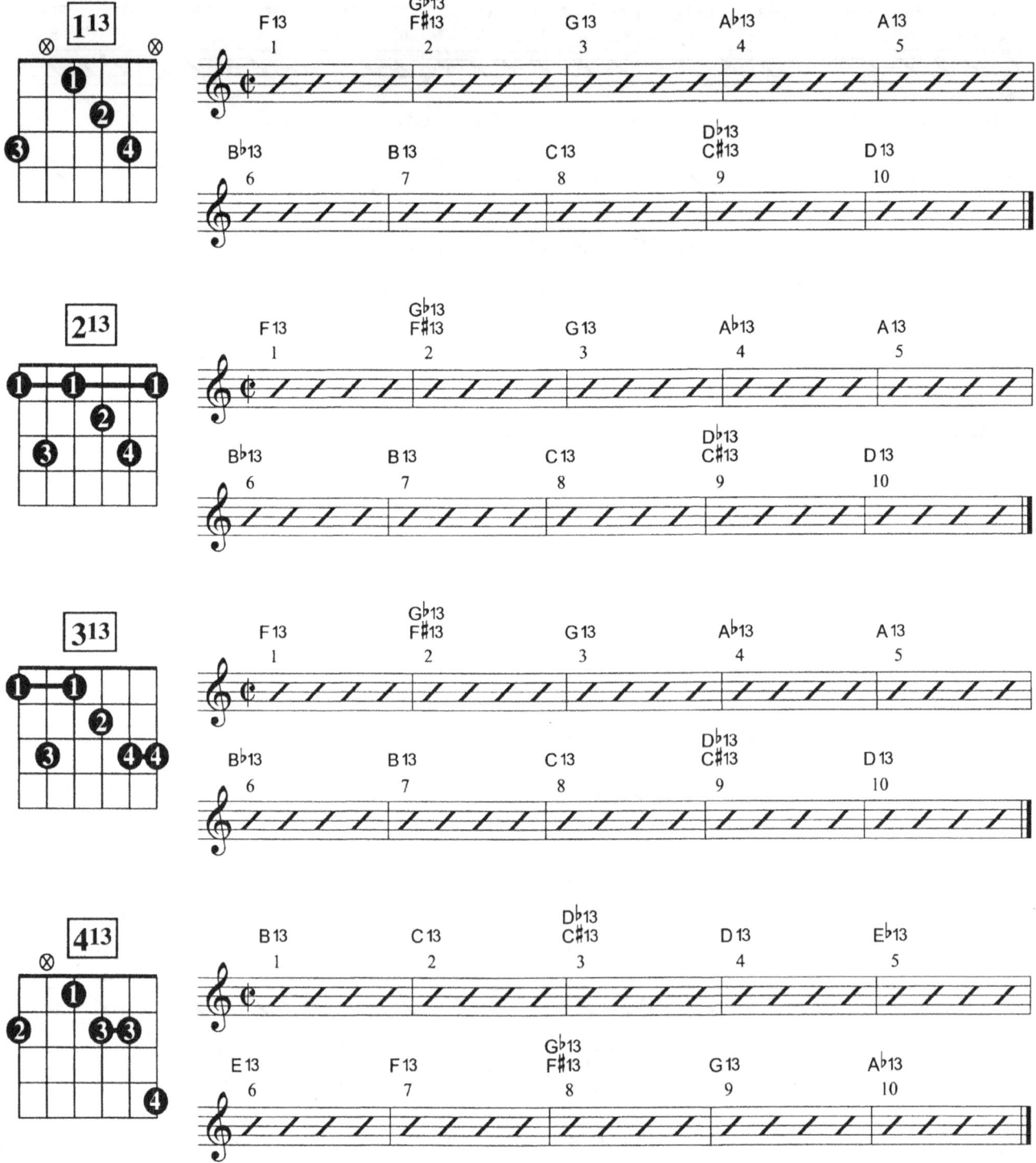

The 13♭9 Chord

Symbol (13♭9) or (13-9) = Thirteen flat nine chord

This chord is made by lowering the 9th tone of the 13th chord a half step, or one fret.

The diamond (♦) indicates the 9th tone. **X** in the 13♭9 form shows original position of the ninth.

X in the circle ⊗ means deadened string. **All six strings are strummed.**

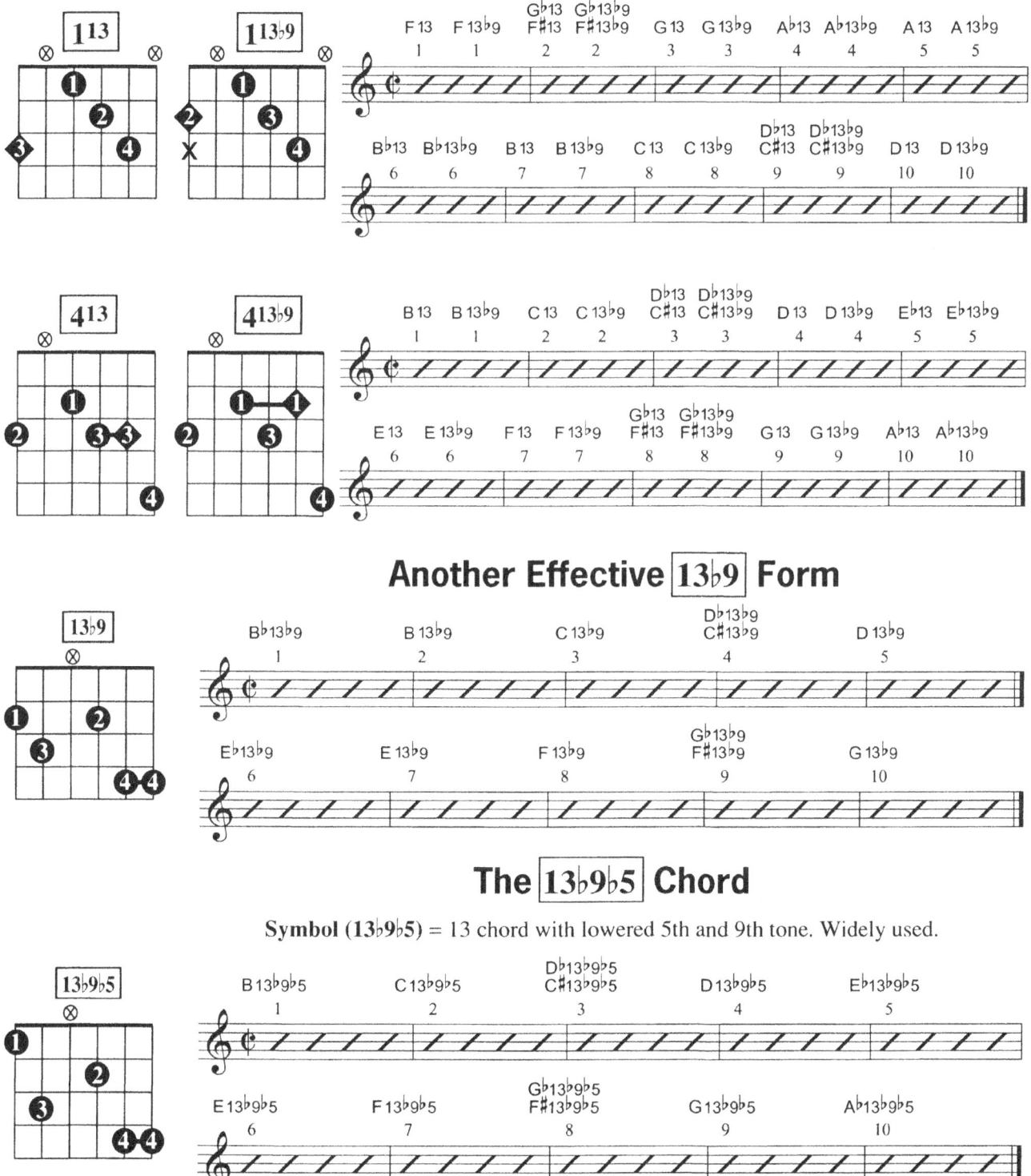

Another Effective 13♭9 Form

The 13♭9♭5 Chord

Symbol (13♭9♭5) = 13 chord with lowered 5th and 9th tone. Widely used.

The $^6_9$ Chord

Symbol ($^6_9$) = Major chord with added 6th and 9th tones

This chord is made by adding the 6th and 9th tones to the major chord.

This chord is used for endings by many modern guitarists.

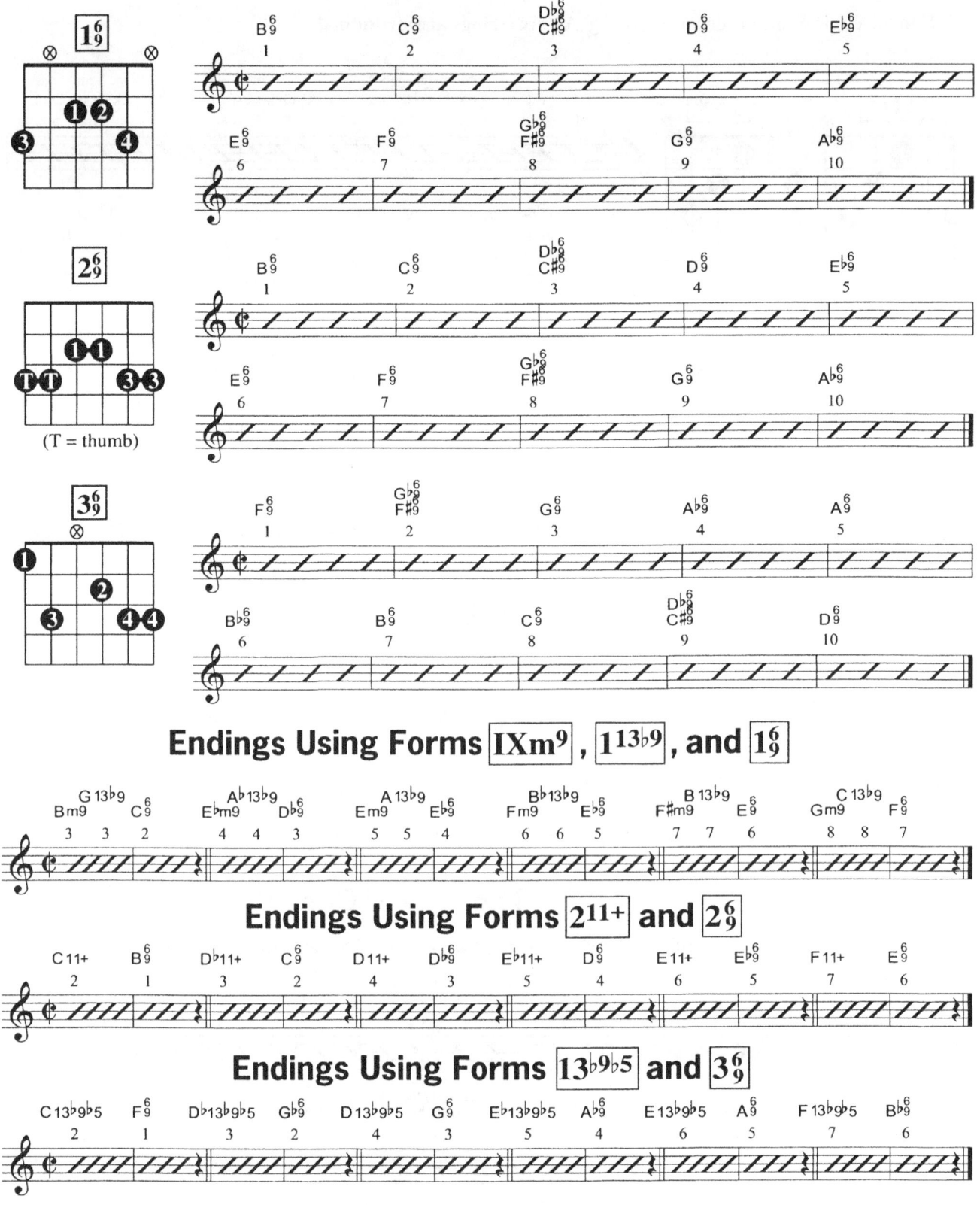

44

Summary for Reference

The chords are derived from the dominant 7th forms $\boxed{I^7}$, $\boxed{III^7}$, $\boxed{V^7}$, and $\boxed{VII^7}$.

All the forms are movable and can be used at the various frets. They should be practiced chromatically up the fingerboard at least to the 10th fret, as shown throughout this system.

• The altered tone is indicated by the diamond (◆). • The **X** shows its former position. • Numbers in the circle (①, ②, etc.) indicates strings. • X in the circle ⊗ indicates deadened string. **All six strings are strummed.**

Chords Derived from Form $\boxed{I^7}$
(Using C7 as an example)

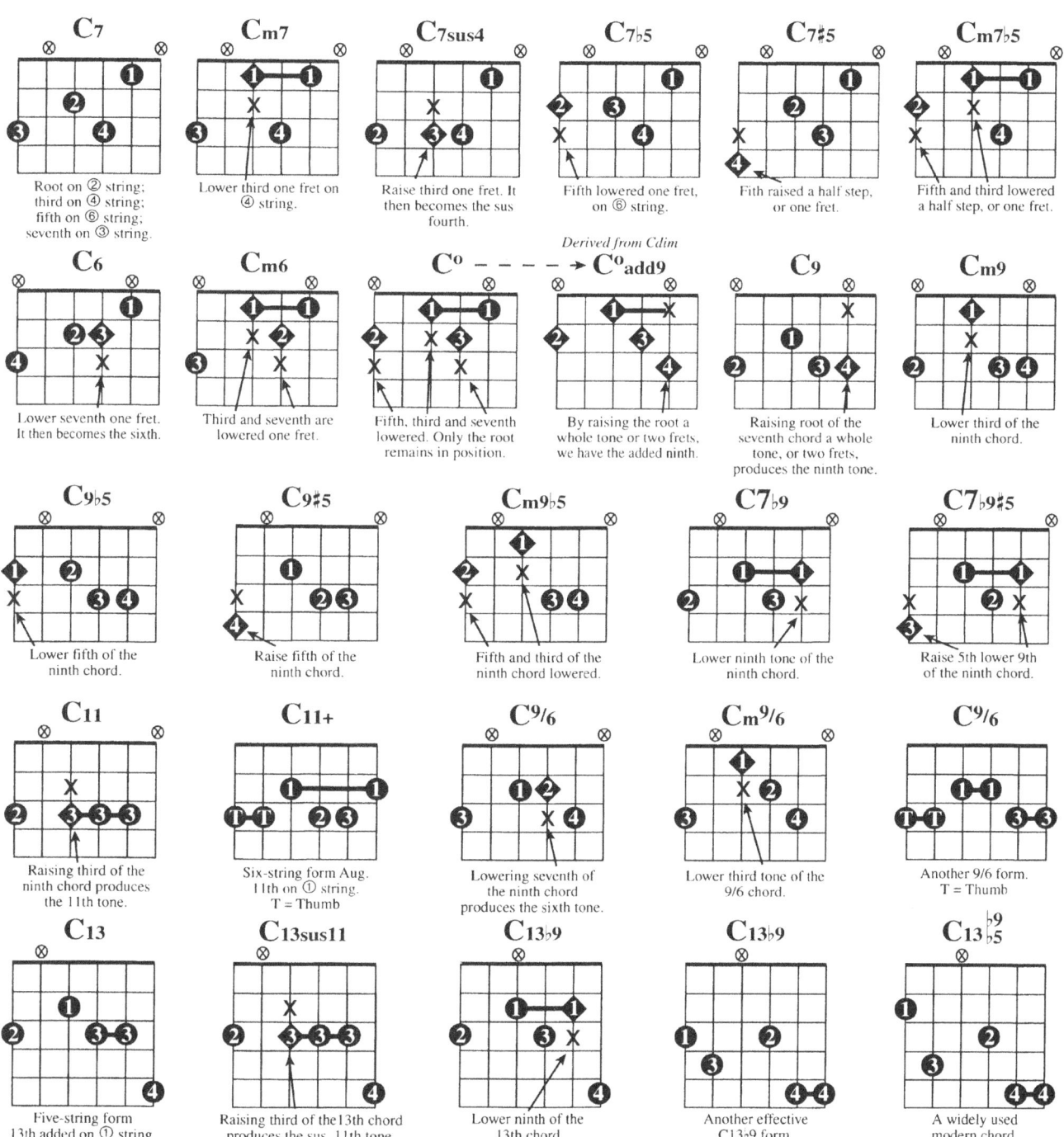

45

Summary for Reference
Chords Derived from Form III⁷
(Using A7 as an example)

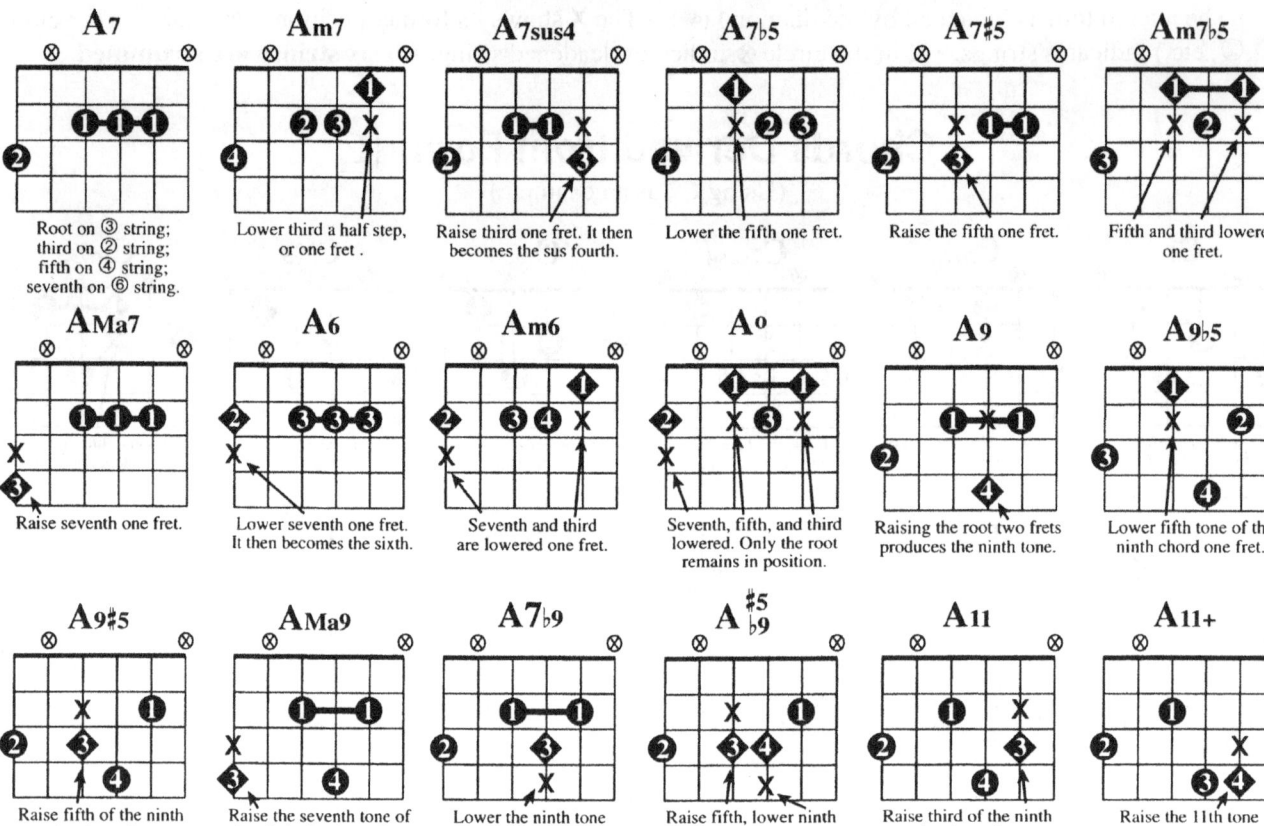

Chords Derived from Form V⁷
(Using G7 as an example)

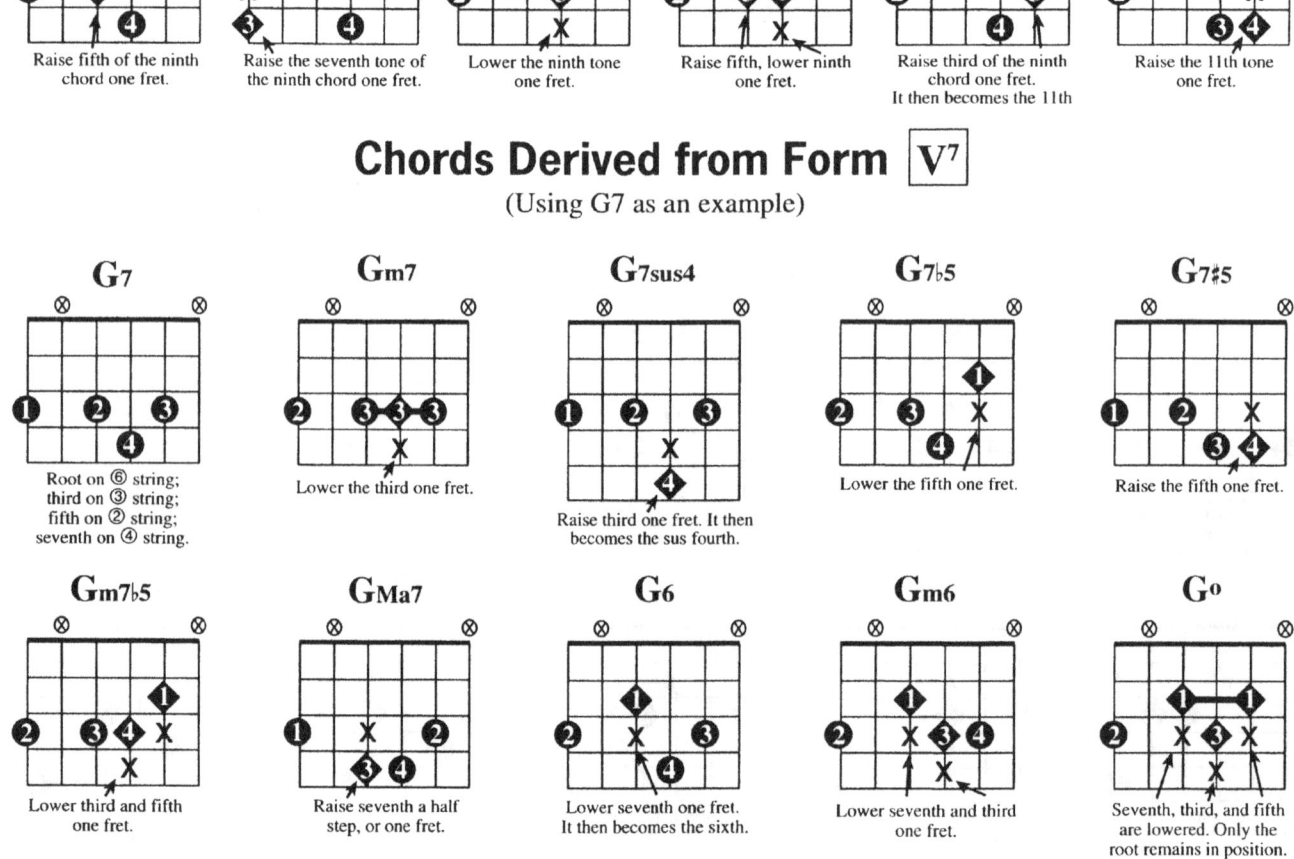

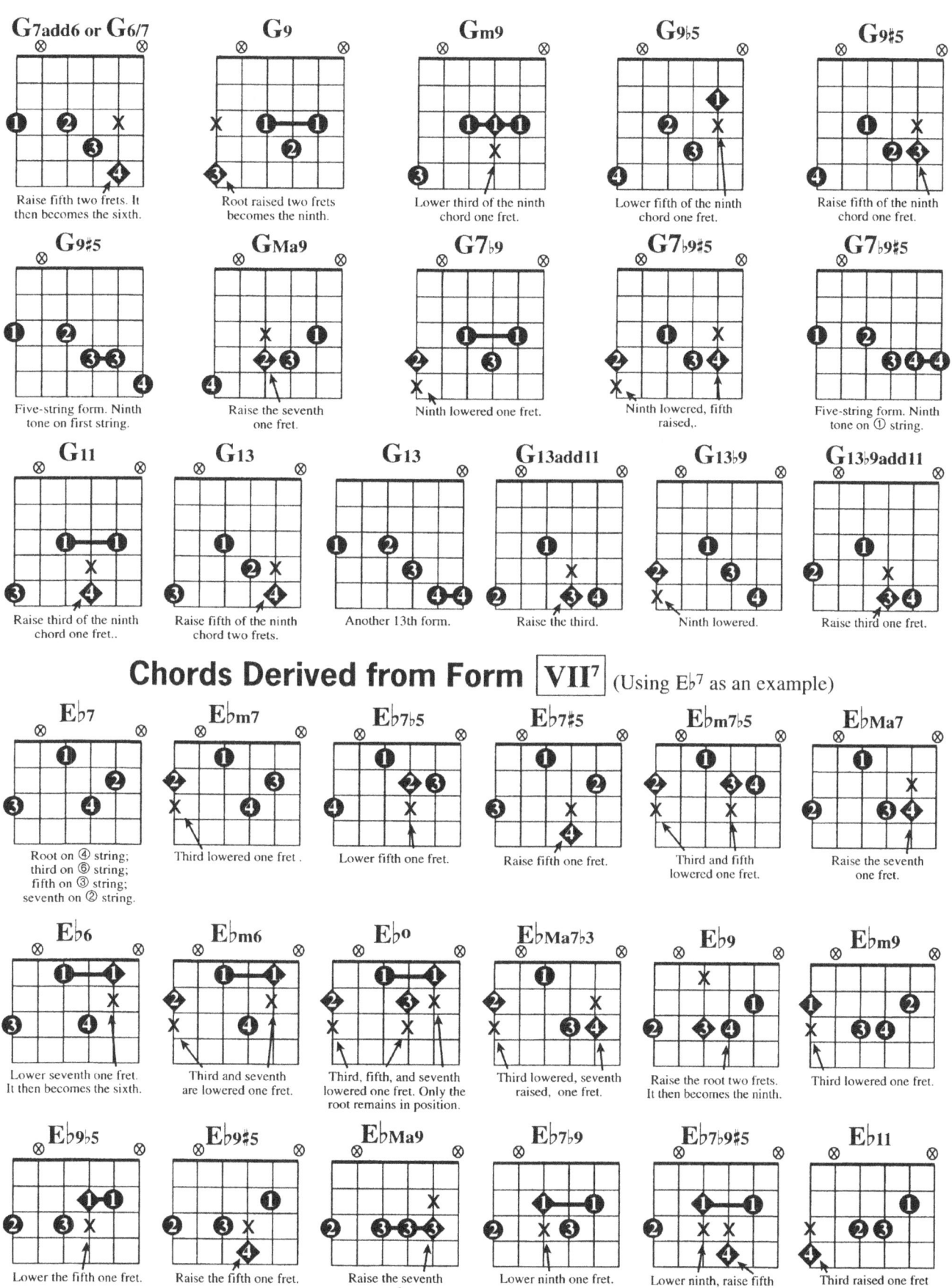

Made in United States
North Haven, CT
16 February 2025